The Rise and Fall of the Southern Tenant Farmers Union in Arkansas

THE RISE AND FALL OF THE SOUTHERN TENANT FARMERS UNION IN ARKANSAS

JAMES D. ROSS JR.

THE UNIVERSITY OF TENNESSEE PRESS / KNOXVILLE

First Edition.

Frontispiece: Sharecropper's shack near West Memphis, Arkansas, from the Library of Congress.

Library of Congress Cataloging-in-Publication Data
Names: Ross, James D., Jr., author.
Title: The rise and fall of the Southern Tenant Farmers Union in Arkansas / James D. Ross Jr.
Description: Knoxville: The University of Tennessee Press, [2017] | Includes bibliographical references and index. |
Identifiers: LCCN 2017027917 (print) | LCCN 2017030873 (ebook) | ISBN 9781621903536 (pdf) | ISBN 9781621903529 (hardcover)
Subjects: LCSH: Southern Tenant Farmers' Union—History. | Tenant farmers—Arkansas—History. | Agricultural laborers—Labor unions—Arkansas—History.
Classification: LCC HD1511.U52 (ebook) | LCC HD1511.U52 R67 2017 (print) | DDC 331.88/130976709043–dc23
LC record available at https://lccn.loc.gov/2017027917

Designed and composed
by Nathan W. Moehlmann,
Goosepen Studio & Press

CONTENTS

ILLUSTRATIONS

FIGURES

TABLES

ACKNOWLEDGMENTS

THIS PROJECT BEGAN ALMOST THIRTY YEARS AGO in Lee William's labor history class at the University of Arkansas at Little Rock. I continued to work on it in Fred William's Arkansas history seminar and in an independent seminar with Charles Bolton. Each of these scholars has effected how I think about history. It was in their classrooms and in their company that I first fell in love with history. Tom Kaiser and Vincent Vinikas both have a great love of history. In their classrooms I watched scholars transform their research into engaging and thought provoking stories that shaped the way I thought about the world and this craft. Each of these scholars taught me to love history and to see it as an act of storytelling.

At the University of Massachusetts at Amherst I had the privilege of writing my master's thesis under the direction of Kevin Boyle. He taught me how to ask tough questions about my sources, and challenged me to become a more conscientious writer. Throughout the years Kevin has asked hard questions about this manuscript and almost anything good in it is a result of his pushing me to be better. Bruce Laurie gave my thesis a careful reading and kept me from making many errors. He also introduced me to many new secondary sources that I would have never found on my own. Manisha Sinha taught me how to think about race and farming in the American South. Her own work has been an inspiration.

At Auburn University, David Harrell carefully read my dissertation and helped me to think more clearly about the nature of religion in the modern South. Larry Gerber read each chapter of this dissertation with a fine eye for detail. He has kept me from making many errors. No one could have a greater dissertation director then Wayne Flynt. When I read his works I knew I wanted to be a historian. He treated me with patience and kindness as I worked through the years to finish the dissertation. He also encouraged me to get the manuscript published. He is a great historian and has not hidden himself away in the academic tower. Instead, he has spent his life not only writing about the most vulnerable, but also in fighting for them in his home state of Alabama. I have sought to follow in his footsteps in Arkansas. He has taught me not only to love history but he has taught me to see the world as it truly is and to fight for justice and equality for all.

Friends and colleagues in Auburn helped in ways I will never be able to repay. Steve Murray was and is a cherished friend. It was through his kindness and gentleness that I made it through graduate school. Jeff Frederick and Scott Billingsly arrived at Auburn as balls of fire. They made me laugh and they made me think more clearly. I will always be thankful for these three friends.

Thomas Wells and his amazing team at the University of Tennessee Press have helped me produce a book I am proud of. Their hard work on the manuscript and their eternal patience with me went beyond the call of duty. I will forever be grateful for their kindness and decency.

Friends in Little Rock kept me going over these last few years. Tim and Tracy Jackson and I have been friends for an eternity already. Over the last few years we have laughed and cried in ways that we could not have when we were young. The last few months talking to their son Sam has renewed my hope in the future we can make. Barclay, Sonya, Langson, and Zora came to Little Rock as my imagination and will were wearing down. They gave me new life, new laughs, and new purpose. They are good people. Kristin Mann has been patient with me and encouraged me in all my endeavors. She is a genuinely good person and a great scholar. Many of my best ideas usually began in an argument or conversation with her. Jennifer, Cary, Cole, and Andi are my family and my friends. We have come to know every intimate detail of each other's lives over these last few years. We have fought and we have laughed together with a depth I have never had before. I could not imagine a day without them. They find this book completely boring and do not even pretend to be interested in it, and for that I love them even more.

Family also supported me, both literally and figuratively. My mother, Susan Ross and sister, Karen Ross have been unfailing supporters, even when I did not deserve it. I will never be able to truly repay them.

Tina has walked beside me for more than thirty years now. I cannot imagine this time without her. She has endured this manuscript in every form. Sometimes with a glad heart, and sometimes threatening to hit me over the head with the computer. I hope when I am one hundred she will still allow me to love her. Madeline, Anna, and Isabella were not even thought of when I began this work. I never thought I could love people as I do them. They too have had to endure a more distant dad than normal.

This book is dedicated to Tina, Madeline, Anna, and Isabella. They are my reason for living. It is in their eyes that I see my worth, and it is in their lives that I want to be.

It is customary in acknowledgments to say that no one but the author is responsible for this work. I have decided to forgo this tradition. All errors and mistakes are the responsibility of Maddie, Anna, Isabella, Cole, and Andi.

INTRODUCTION

PRESBYTERIAN PASTOR AND SOMETIME THEOLOGIAN Frederick Buechner once argued:

> At its heart theology, like most fiction, is essentially autobiography. Aquinas, Calvin, Barth, Tillich, working out their systems in their own ways and in their own language, are all telling us the stories of their lives, and if you press them far enough, even at their most cerebral and forbidding, you find an experience of flesh and blood, a human face smiling or frowning or weeping or covering its eyes before something that happened once. What happened once may be no more than a child falling sick, a thunderstorm, a dream, and yet it made for the face and inside the face a difference which no theology can ever entirely convey or entirely conceal.[1]

I do not know if this is true for theology or fiction, but it does ring true to my commitment to this book. I became interested in the Southern Tenant Farmers' Union (STFU) before I even knew the union existed. At the feet of my grandmother, from my earliest days, I heard stories of picking cotton. She had been a sharecropper from the early 1920s until she was forced to leave the farm in the mid-1960s. She mixed her stories of pulling a cotton sack up a hot and seemingly endless cotton row with images and words from her oversized King James Bible. To her, Jesus, Moses, and the Apostle John were as real and present as her closest friends. It was in their words of a new heaven and new earth where there would be no tears or sorrow or suffering that she saw and understood her world. She was never bitter for not owning any land or even a house; she simply sat in her chair waiting on her children and grandchildren to visit so she could tell more stories and sing songs of Jesus' love and of her home in heaven. Little did I know that she was giving me the background to understand the men and women who made up the STFU.

At the same time I came to know my grandmother's sister, that everyone said was crazy. She would visit from time to time from the exotic world of California, and at her feet I heard radically different stories. She had left the farm in 1934 and gone to California where she started picking peaches. When the Congress of Industrial Organizations (CIO) began to organize peach pickers she was one of the first to join, and over time she became an organizer. She believed in unions; she believed in the collective power of workers to change the world. From my "crazy" great-aunt I learned stories of people who believed in something strong enough to die for it. Little did I know she was preparing me to understand the men and women who made up the STFU.

Sitting in college in the mid-1980s I heard a professor tell the story of the STFU, and I quickly began to devour everything I could find on the union. By the early 1990s, I thought I understood all there was to know about the union. Then I discovered that H. L. Mitchell, the union's secretary, had spent years collecting the papers of the STFU on microfilm and I began a twenty-year study of the letters that rank and file members of the union wrote to union officials, government leaders, and others. As I studied these letters the union took on a life of its own, and I realized I wanted to add the voices of the men and women who created the union back to their rightful place in the union's history.

One might ask, "Is there a need for a new history of the Southern Tenant Farmers' Union?" Donald Grubbs's wonderful institutional history of the union, published almost fifty years ago has stood the test of time as a wonderful narrative. But my reading of the sources has led me to see the origin of the union, the participation of the Socialist Party, the alleged racial harmony, and the role of religion differently from Grubbs. These interpretive differences, plus the availability of new sources leads me to believe that it is time to take a new look at the STFU.

A recent article in the Arkansas *Democrat-Gazette* shows the importance of taking a fresh look at the Union. One historian was quoted as saying that the alleged racial unity within the STFU was "one of those important moments, not just in the history of the South but in the history of the United States, when people were able to work together." But what if this narrative is not the story of the STFU? What if the story of the STFU is in fact the story of the South and of the United States?[2]

Participants in the union, social critics, and historians have wrestled with the meaning of the STFU since the 1930s. Many scholars concerned with the growth of unions and social movements have been drawn to the STFU because of its seemingly bizarre story: a socialist-led union in the heart of the traditionally conservative South. Historical interpretation of the STFU has gone through two phases. In the 1960s a group of "New Left" historians saw the union as a radical force pushing the New Deal to the left. In the 1980s a newer group of historians reversed the interpretation, viewing the New Deal as progressive in the context of Southern history and the STFU as a conservative force trying to preserve the past.

H. L. Mitchell, the union's secretary, was the first to write a history of the STFU. A socialist and a businessman, Mitchell began to write a history of the union in the 1930s, but laid it aside for the more pressing work of organizing and managing the union. In the 1960s and 1970s, Mitchell began to lecture about the union's past and developed a history of the STFU that viewed the Union as a radical force that had a chance to construct a new America in the southern cotton fields. According to Mitchell, the union was a precursor to the Civil Rights Movement of the 1950s and 1960s. He wanted the union remembered for its radicalism and what he called its interracial quality. Mitchell was so caught up in his own commitment to socialism and anti-racist organizations that he at times forgot that the sharecroppers and tenant farmers expressed themselves in different ways from their leaders.[3]

Mitchell wrote many narratives about the union. In the earliest narratives Mitchell's story involves many different voices all working to build a strong union. Sometimes those voices were in harmony; at other times the discord almost destroyed the union. In later narratives, Mitchell simplified the story to a few people doing most of the union's work. If we are to truly understand the STFU we need to restore Mitchell's original understanding of the union's complexities. The union was not the work of a few socialist leaders; instead, it was made up of a multiplicity of competing voices.

Subsequent works on the STFU by historians associated with the student upheaval in the 1960s repeated Mitchell's view of the union.[4] The majority of these authors stressed the heroic action of the union's leaders in the face of horrific violence. The union was portrayed as a socialist critic of the New Deal, and the STFU was seen as offering an alternative vision for the South. One enthusiastic proponent of this perspective went so far as to argue, "Beginning as a critic of the New Deal agriculture programs, [the STFU] grew into a mass movement which aimed at the reconstruction of southern agriculture along socialist lines and the elimination of the political and educational disabilities which made poor white and black passive observers of their own exploitation."[5] These works tend to be good sources for explaining many of the views of the STFU's socialist and communist leadership. But when it comes to examining what the rank and file were saying, they are inadequate.[6]

In the 1980s the STFU was reinterpreted in a new light. Historian Pete Daniel argued that the STFU was a conservative reaction to the radical upheaval caused by the changes New Deal policies wrought. Daniel argued that the sharecroppers and tenant farmers were better off with the death of the sharecropping and tenant farming system. This is undeniable, but it begs a central question: what did the ending of the sharecropping and tenant farming system mean to the men and women who joined the union? This newer interpretation is inadequate because it, like the earlier interpretations, does not examine the thoughts of the rank and file at that pivotal moment of change.[7]

These two schools, one which sees the STFU as essentially radical and the other which sees it as essentially conservative, share a common inadequacy in not considering the views of the sharecroppers and tenant farmers. None of these works examine the thousands of letters in the STFU archives from the Union's rank and file. Only by examining these letters can we begin to understand what many sharecroppers and tenant farmers were thinking and feeling when they joined the union. This book, while deeply influenced by Pete Daniel's work, attempts to add the voices of the sharecroppers and tenant farmers who worked to make the STFU their organization.

In examining the letters of sharecroppers and tenant farmers the conservative/radical paradigm is not sufficient to explain why the sharecroppers and tenant farmers joined the Union and subsequently what the union meant to them. Instead, the STFU must be seen in the light of the long history of southern radicalism beginning with Reconstruction and moving through the Farmers' Alliance and populism. As Lawrence Goodwyn has argued, this southern radicalism was not socialism, nor was it communism. Instead, it held to the idea of fighting for individual property rights with collective action. The former slaves struggled together to secure land to farm; white and black farmers in the 1880s and 1890s fought the interests of capital that they believed were attempting to steal their land.[8]

These movements were linked by the members' commitment to private land ownership. The idea that only a man who owned land was free died hard with these poor southerners, white and black. The men and women who joined the STFU sought two goals. First they wanted their immediate needs met. They could not live without food and without shelter. They had always attempted to help one another. The union helped focus this tradition of reciprocity into a mass collective action. They also had a vision for their own future. These sharecroppers and tenant farmers wanted to own their own land. They repeatedly made this clear to the union leadership.

What is needed is a more holistic approach to the STFU. In the past fifty years the hard work of historians has given us a sufficient understanding of the radical leadership of the STFU. What we now must do is integrate the wishes, dreams, and ideology of the rank and file with that of the leadership. When this is done it is obvious that the radicalism of the leaders was not always mirrored in the words and actions of the rank and file. While the white leaders may have expressed a commitment to racial justice, white members often did not. While the union's socialist and communist leaders may have hoped for cooperative land ownership, the members often did not. There was a strong divide between the goals of the leaders and the goals of the rank and file.

Before we can understand the union we must first examine who the sharecroppers and tenant farmers were and what they believed before they joined the STFU. In examining the counties in Arkansas that would eventually be dominated by the STFU and comparing it to other counties in Arkansas and the surrounding states, we begin to see that the men and women who joined the STFU were in the most desperate and distressing position of any sharecroppers and tenant farmers in the South. In comparing statistical data and textual evidence we find that the men and women who met on the plantation in Arkansas to found the Union were at their wit's end, and most viewed the union as their last, best hope.

In the traditional narrative of the STFU the union's founding was almost accidental. Sharecroppers and tenant farmers meeting on a plantation had invited two socialist businessmen to one of their meetings. At that meeting it was decided to ask the two socialists to help form a union that would organize all sharecroppers regardless of race. But the real story is far more complex. When these sharecroppers and tenant farmers met to found the union, they soon discovered that the people they sat down with had very different agendas. Historians like Donald Grubbs and others argued that the eighteen sharecroppers and tenant farmers meeting at Sunnyside School in 1934 founded the union. In one respect they are right, there was a meeting at the Sunnyside School that Mitchell always claimed was where the STFU was founded. In examining the papers of Clay East, the other socialist businessman involved in the early days of the STFU, we must push the founding of the union back to the spring of 1933. In the traditional narrative, H. L. Mitchell is sometimes presented as a swashbuckling hero, but it is important to remember that he was only twenty-four years old and very new to the political game. He made many mistakes that can be attributed to his youth. His vision of the coming revolution was as dogmatic as any of the rank and file's religious fundamentalism and would put him into conflict with his new partners in founding the union—the Socialist Party of America. The Socialist Party had a massive influence in the founding of the union by providing money, leadership, vision, and motivation. The founding of the union was a very complex event. The sharecroppers and tenant farmers, the Socialist Party of America, H. L. Mitchell, and Clay East each had differing agendas that must be unraveled to truly understand the union.

Even as we unravel the complex origins of the union, we still are left wondering why white and black sharecroppers and tenant farmers would join the STFU. The sharecroppers and tenant farmers left thousands of letters that let us see into the world of their fears and dreams. They proved to be a very articulate group of people. In their letters we find not only their hopes and dreams, but also their critique of the sharecropping system and the New Deal. These men and women devoutly followed fundamentalist and Pentecostal Christianity. This rural religion was the language that these men and women mobilized to attack the injustices of the plantation system and to offer solutions to those injustices. The language of the Bible was like the oxygen around them, which they used to analyze their world. In many ways the history of the STFU is the history of poor people using anything at their disposal—religion, politics, and a sense of community—to protect and sustain their families. Their critique and the answer they offered where full of hope. They believed the Kingdom of God could be established on the earth, and they believed that the STFU was the vehicle to bring that about. The meaning of the union for different groups was also complex. This story of multiple meanings must be unraveled if the STFU is to be understood.

In the end, historians are faced with one glaring question: If the union began with so much hope in 1934, why did it end in such misery by 1945? The reality was that the sharecroppers and tenant farmers began to leave the union as early as 1937, and by 1938 there was not much of a rank and file to speak of in Arkansas. While violence and mechanization (especially the coming of the tractor) are important factors in the demise of the union, it cannot be understated that the union's original pluralism in vision led to internal tensions between the rank and file and the union leadership over questions of land ownership, practical daily needs, and the meaning of mechanization. These differences in goals and tactics greatly contributed to the union' demise.

But sadly, and most importantly, racial tension and questions over the use of violence within STFU locals would lead to the ultimate demise of the STFU. The original members were strongly committed to the racial integration of the union, but soon after the union began to expand problems arose. In November 1935, H. L. Mitchell wrote to Nathan Wiley to remind him "it is very important that we organize the whites as well as the Negroes." In the letter Mitchell is insistent that the union be integrated. Donald H. Grubs argues that when the union reached the large towns where blacks and whites did not have such intimate contact it was impossible to organize interracial locals.[9] But beyond the geography of the small towns, there was white opposition to working with black members in the locals. The racism was not just isolated to the rank and file. African American leaders were never comfortable with Mitchell's racial paternalism. These African American leaders, many of them preachers, believed they should lead the Union. The union was destroyed by racism of both the white leaders and the white rank and file.

Mitchell used to love talking about the non-violent nature of the union, but again the reality within the union was far more complex. Sharecroppers and tenant farmers sometimes reacted to the massive violence that was brought against them by planters and local police. Sometimes sharecroppers and tenant farmers would react with stoicism; sometimes they would run away; and sometimes to the horror of the leadership they would arm themselves for violent confrontation. Again it is essential to see that the union was not unified by race and pacifism, as many historians have claimed. Nor was the union without internal strife. These issues would contribute to the STFU's early demise.

This book is not a detailed history of the STFU. Instead, it is an examination of how the union was founded, what it meant to those who joined, and why it died so quickly. These questions are the ones that have been overly romanticized in the past, and if we are to ever have a new systemic history of the STFU then we must set the record straight on these questions. These questions also have much to teach us as we struggle in our own day to form meaningful movements to bring change to our bent, bruised, and broken world.

At the end of his life, Herbert Gutman was concerned about the trend of some social historians who had produced minute and romanticized studies of working people's lives. In one of the last pieces he wrote, Gutman warned historians not to "argue that exploited and subordinate men and women make history, but [to see that] they regularly participate in and help shape significant historical processes."[10] To the men and women who joined the STFU this was one of the most significant things they ever did. Restoring their voices to the history of the 1930s is imperative if we are to understand the full development of the South during the Great Depression.

CHAPTER ONE

BY THE TIME IRENE ROBERTSON of the Work's Project Administration writing staff caught up with John Wells in the late 1930s he was in his early eighties, but he clearly recalled his childhood in slavery. He was born in Edmonson, Arkansas, on Henry Edmonson's farm in the mid-1850s. Wells remembered that when the Civil War approached Arkansas, he and the other Edmondson slaves were sent to safety on a Texas farm. After the war he and other former slaves migrated back to Edmondson and found that their former master and his family had died in a yellow fever epidemic that swept over the region. The former slaves settled on the land that had been their master's and over the years, it became theirs. With the passage of time, these former slaves and their children created a vibrant town of African-American businessmen and farm owners. But in the early 1930s most of these black landowners lost their land to a large white landowner from a nearby town. In a few short years after the depression of 1929, these former slaves turned landowners entered the rank of sharecroppers and tenant farmers. Wells told the interviewer that day that "things not going like it ought somehow."[1]

Ida Davis was born in 1906 in an old lumber camp to which her father had migrated in 1899 from the Indian Territory. Before moving to the camp, William Davis, her father, had farmed as a small landowner. The Davis' had been, so Ida related, on the move almost every generation. If one traced the family back along the male line, one would eventually come to John Davis who lived in Virginia in the 1790s and owned eight slaves. In the 1930s Ida Davis was a long way from the yeoman farmers or small plantation landowners who were her ancestors. She had been married at sixteen and by 1935 had five of her six children. She and her husband Silas tenant farmed land owned by her father, who was an unscrupulous man willing to do anything to protect his property and wealth. In later years he would even have Ida's husband, his son-in-law, murdered because he had campaigned for a man running for sheriff who had not been approved by Bill Davis, and because Silas wanted to move his family to another farm to work.[2]

John Wells and Ida Davis both lived through times of great change. From slave to landowner to sharecropper, John Wells exemplified these changes as they were experienced by a generation of African-Americans. He carried deep within him the hopes of landownership and economic power promised in the post Civil War era, and all the sorrows of the betrayal of those promises. Ida Davis also exemplified something of the changes as they were experienced by rural whites. She carried deep within her the memories of large landownership, yet she spent her days working as a tenant farmer trying to achieve the status her ancestors had before her.

At the end of the Civil War, men and women found themselves sharecropping and tenant farming across the South for various reasons. For African-Americans, sharecropping and tenant farming developed over time as a compromise between their desire for landownership and the labor needs of their former masters. As northern troops moved through the plantation areas of the South, many slaves joined the troops either to fight for their freedom or to find safety for themselves and their families. Former slaves began almost immediately to try to obtain land for themselves and their families, believing that because they had worked the land for so long it was theirs by right. After Union troops gained control of more of the South, some slaves began to take the land that their former masters had abandoned as they fled advancing Union troops. Some freed people even divided the land among themselves and planted gardens to support themselves and their families.

When the war ended, many Southern plantation owners returned and took control of their land from their former slaves. Landlords attempted to install a gang labor system, but the freed people were never happy with this labor system because it reminded them too much of the slave labor system they had endured for so many generations. Most freed people refused to work in gangs. New landlords and their former slaves both needed a way to make a living and were forced to make compromises. Former slave owners needed someone to work their fields and former slaves needed a way to support their families. Former slaves and the plantation owners experimented with a number of different ways to organize work. In his study of Freedman's Bureau reports and labor contracts between freed people and plantation owners, Ralph Shomowitz has found that there were at least seven ways the two parties attempted to organize their work: standing wages, share of the crop, sharing of time, standing rent, wages in kind, money payment per task, and various explicit incentive schemes.[3] As freed people and new landlords struggled over how best to organize labor in the cotton fields, the country was entering a period some historians call Radical Reconstruction. During this time, as former slaves became more involved in the political process, they continued their struggle for control of their lives.

By 1880 the options had narrowed severely: sharecropping and standing rents became the dominant forms of labor organization in the plantation South. In the formation of these two labor systems neither tenants nor landowners had completely gained what they sought. The landlord gained field workers who would be legally bound to share the risk of planting crops. The former freedmen who struggled for these two forms of labor organization after they realized that land redistribution was not going to occur gained a certain amount of freedom from their former masters.[4]

Whites, meanwhile, came to sharecropping and tenant farming by two different routes. In their research on Georgia, historians Frederick Bode and Donald Ginger suggested that many white southerners were involved in tenant farming in the antebellum period. In Georgia these two historians found that in 1860 tenancy rates were lowest on the older cotton lands of the lower Eastern piedmont and in the yeomanry dominated regions of the wiregrass. On newer cotton lands to the west, ante-bellum tenancy rates averaged in the upper twenty percent range. Tenancy rates rose to thirty percent and more on the cotton frontier of the southwest and on the cotton fringes of the upper Piedmont. And in the higher mountains and on the palmetto flats along the Florida border tenancy rates exceeded forty percent.[5] They conclude from their study of the population and agricultural census of 1860 that "a substantial number of white farmers did not own their land." If Bode and Ginger's work is accurate, many late nineteenth century tenants may have simply persisted from the ante-bellum period.[6]

Historian Steven Hahn has located another route that whites took to tenant farming. In his research on the Georgia upcountry Hahn found that many whites descended from yeomen farming to the emotionally and financially devastating position of tenant farming or sharecropping. Hahn found that with changes in market relations after the Civil War debts that had traditionally linked upcountry white yeomen together in an "intricate network of social relations" began to "provoke tensions and conflicts."[7] In the financial upheaval of the Reconstruction period, Hahn explained, creditors began to call in their debts, even going so far as to use auction blocks to sell yeomen farmers' lands who could not pay their debts. As staple crops moved upcountry, former small landowners soon became landless sharecroppers on large plantations.[8]

As conservative leaders ended Radical Reconstruction, Southern politicians began to rewrite the laws that gave legal primacy to sharecroppers and tenant farmers. Lien laws were quickly overturned to return the advantage on the lien to the landowner. Sharecropping and tenant farming began to lose the degree of freedom that made it attractive to many African Americans. For many whites, tenancy was quickly changing from a stepping stone to landownership into a permanent condition. Because of laws created by Redeemer governments the tenant system degraded into a system of oppressive debt peonage.[9]

From 1880 to 1920, tenant farms spread rapidly across the South. Although tenancy was on the increase nation-wide, the South experienced an astonishing growth. [See Table 1] As the laws passed by Redeemer governments began to take effect and cotton staple crop agriculture began to spread, more and more small farmers became sharecroppers and tenant farmers. The 1,231,144 sharecropper and tenant farms that existed in 1900 made up about forty-seven percent of all southern farms and about twenty-two percent of all United States farms. Tenant farms outside the South in the same year made up about fourteen percent of all United States farms.

TABLE 1. PERCENTAGE GROWTH OF TENANT FARMS, 1880–1920

South	187.28
Non-South	83.47
United States	139.59

Source: Statistical History of the United States from Colonial Times to the Present

As southern tenancy grew, its production center shifted from the southeast to the southwest. By the 1910 census, cotton production had already begun to move from the old eastern cotton growing areas to the southwest. Historian Pete Daniel has shown that between 1910 and 1930 Texas and Oklahoma doubled their cotton acreage. At the same time Mississippi, Arkansas, and Louisiana increased their acreage by forty percent, while Alabama, Georgia, and South and North Carolina only increased their cotton acreage by five percent. Daniel showed that in the eastern cotton belt production declined from twelve million acres in 1910–1914 to 8.8 million in 1922. To the west, in the Mississippi delta, acreage rose from 6.6 million in 1921 to 11.1 million in 1930.[10]

Into this new southwestern cotton land, in a small town in northeastern Arkansas, a small group of men and women who had spent their lives sharecropping and tenant farming, would form a union to attempt to gain control over their destinies. Why would these men and women in this area rise up to challenge the status quo? What conditions would set the stage and make it plausible for thousands of poor white and black sharecroppers and tenant farmers to join the Southern Tenant Farmers' Union?

This movement of cotton production west was caused, in part, by the promise of fresh land free from the ravages of planting without proper fertilizer or erosion control. The boll weevil also contributed to this move west. As the boll weevil entered the east from south Texas it made much of the land unprofitable. But as Pete Daniel has shown the boll weevil did very little damage in the Mississippi delta, leaving this land safe for profitable cultivation.[11]

The state of Arkansas benefited from this move of cotton production westward. From 1880–1910 the population of Arkansas grew by a little over ninety-six percent; from 1910 to 1930 the state's population grew by almost one-hundred-seventy-eight percent. A comparison of national and southeastern population patterns, for the same period shows that Arkansas' population grew far faster than either.[12] [See Table 2]

TABLE 2. POPULATION GROWTH

	Arkansas	Southeast	United States
1880–1910	96.18%	33%	83.55%
1910–1930	177.86%	23.55%	33.31%

Source: Statistical History of the United States from Colonial Times to the Present

If population in the Arkansas delta cotton growing counties is compared to the state's non-delta counties, we can see that the majority of the Arkansas growth from 1910–1930 occurred in those counties washed by the swift currents of the Mississippi River. Non-delta areas grew by a mere six percent, while the delta counties grew by thirty-three percent.[13] During the nineteenth century the upper counties in this delta region of Arkansas had for the most part been a swampland. The improved farm land for these ten upper counties in 1900 stood at 807,897 acres. From 1900 to 1910 improved land in these counties increased a little more than fifty-seven percent; from 1910 to 1920 it increased by almost another twelve percent.[14]

What accounted for such large growth? One of the main reasons was the drainage work done by Arthur E. Morgan. Morgan was born in Ohio in 1878. Shortly thereafter his family moved to St. Cloud, Minnesota where John Morgan, Arthur's father, opened a small engineering business. At an early age Arthur went to work for his father digging ditches. According to Morgan's biographer, Morgan's father taught Arthur how to "shoot elevations with a transit and to lay lines for ditches and levees."[15] This was all the training Morgan had to become a hydraulic engineer. He went to work for the federal government in the conservation movement that Theodore Roosevelt had promoted, and in 1908 Morgan took over a government drainage project that ran from Missouri to Louisiana.[16] Two years later he completed his work on the upper Arkansas delta.[17] "I had dreams," Morgan wrote in 1972, "of that rich land becoming the site of prosperous homes for many farmers."[18] Morgan's dream of small farms scattered throughout northeastern Arkansas was never fulfilled. As he acknowledged in 1972, "lumber interests" had bought up most profitable land and turned it into large plantations worked by thousands of tenant farmers. Between 1910 and 1930 the number of tenant farms in the Arkansas delta increased by a little over seventy-seven percent. In the counties that would eventually have STFU branches, the number of tenant farms increased by a little more than sixty-eight percent. And in the five counties that would eventually have the largest number of STFU locals, the number of tenant farms increased by more than one-hundred-thirty-seven percent. With what must have been a lifetime of regret, Morgan confessed, "You can imagine my disappointment at seeing this outcome of my drainage work."[19]

Life for these northwest Arkansas sharecroppers and tenant farmers made them dependent on other people's honesty and integrity. Each year sharecroppers and tenant farmers contracted with landowners. They would provide labor in exchange for a percentage of the crop.

The work was hard. Fields were prepared and cotton planted. During the rainy season, tenants hoed grass and weeds. Then cotton was "laid by" in August and work slowed down. In September at cotton picking time the workday became longer and the work much more arduous. One sharecropper described the work: "Cotton picking is here now. That means that all of us must go to the fields. Young and old; men and women and children. We will drag heavy sacks down the long rows. They get heavier as the long day goes on. It is backbreaking toil. This year they plan to do the same. A good picker will average about 100 pounds per day throughout the season. Women and children still less."[20]

At the end of the season, when the landlord balanced the books, sharecropper and tenant farmer families were paid whatever was due them. A 1933–34 report prepared by the Memphis, Tennessee chapter of the League for Industrial Democracy, headed by biologist William Amberson, found that on average families in northeastern Arkansas made $262.00 per year.[21] This sum was inadequate for a family to live. Sharecropping and tenant farming consequently lived lifestyles where extreme debt and dependence on others was common.

Because sharecroppers and tenant farmers usually exhausted their small earnings from the previous crop, plantation owners usually furnished food, seed, and supplies that would later be deducted from the sharecroppers and tenant farmers' share of the crop. This system allowed some plantation owners to cheat sharecroppers and tenant farmers. The Amberson study found in one small eastern Arkansas town that food coming from the plantation store was priced higher than that found in non-plantation stores.[22] Because this money was being subtracted from sharecropper and tenant farmers' incomes, provisions from company stores were inadequate for good health and decent life. According to Franzier Hunt writing in the *New York World-Telegram* in 1935, sharecroppers and tenant farmers ate salt pork, corn bread, and molasses for most meals.[23]

The year 1914 would change the cotton South forever. While sharecroppers and tenant farmers were streaming onto Arkansas lands and the other states west of Alabama, the world was plunged into war. Before 1914, the South faced two foes: the boll weevil and the tendency of farmers to produce more cotton than the world market could absorb. Between 1890–1920, as the boll weevil moved across the South, it left behind a trail of devastation "wider than Sherman's army."[24] Farmers stood by and watched helplessly as a tiny insect destroyed a lifetime of work. Both state and federal governments failed to respond adequately. As Pete Daniel pointed out, "state governments refused to quarantine infested areas, and the federal government proved loath to interfere with interstate commerce, even the possible ruin of it."[25]

Bad economic choices likewise devastated the region. One of the eternal curses of the cotton South had been farmers' assumptions that the way to make more money when cotton prices were up was to plant more cotton. The reality was overproduction which drove cotton prices down. From 1876 onward, cotton prices had remained below fifteen cents per pound.[26]

For several years before 1914 cotton prices fell below the cost of production, but all of this quickly changed in 1914. The European war helped create an overwhelming demand for cotton as international cotton production ground to a halt just as countries at war needed increased amounts of cotton for war materials. It fell to American farmers to fill international markets. The six years between 1914 and 1920 consequently were a very profitable time for cotton producers. As Table 4 shows, cotton prices rose from 7.35 cents per pound in 1914 to 35.34 cents per pound in 1919. With this new money cotton farmers invested in new land, some took on new tenants, and

TABLE 3. COTTON PRICE PER POUND, 1877–1914

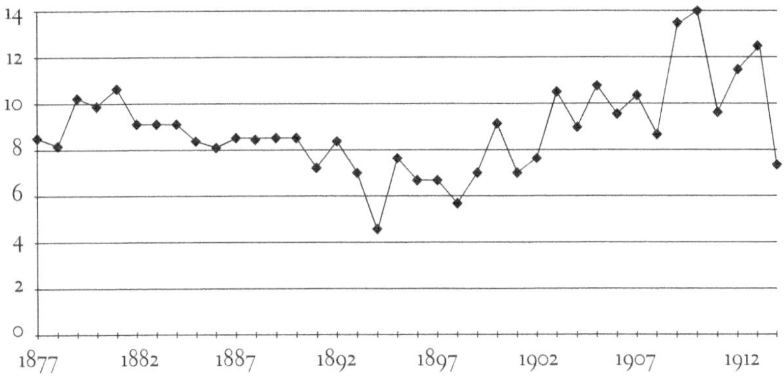

Source: Statistical History of the United States from Colonial Times to the Present

TABLE 4. COTTON PRICE PER POUND, 1910–1919

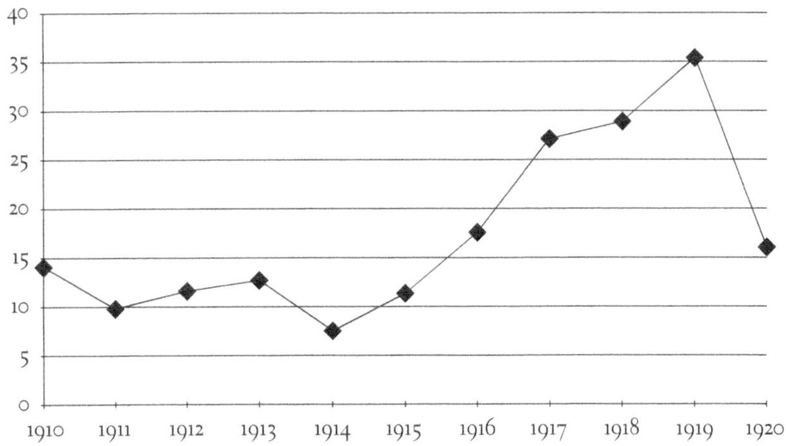

Source: Statistical History of the United States from Colonial Times to the Present

a few even invested in machinery. Farmers were also able to get mortgages on their farms to purchase more land. But the war could not last forever.

Southern cotton farmers had increased production each year of the war, but in 1920 the bottom fell out of cotton prices. That year the price of cotton per pound plummeted to 15.89 cents, a drop of a little over fifty-five percent, and although the price went up in the mid-1920s, it soon plummeted again.[27] Historians have generally traced two reasons for this decline. After the World War ended, international cotton producers could again begin planting and trading cotton. This new cotton glutted the world market and began to eat into southern farmer's profits. DuPont and Celanese Corporation of America, moreover, began to produce synthetic cloth made from chemicals. These synthetic materials proved to be as durable as cotton and, as historian Thomas Clark has noted, they "knew no drouth, no insects, no ravaging plant diseases."[28] This double punch particularly devastated small farmers, many of whom had taken loans and new mortgages based on anticipated growth in the price of cotton.

With this drop in cotton prices the number of cotton farm owners began to decline. From 1920 to 1930, there was a decrease in southern cotton farm ownership of a little over fifteen percent. During this same period tenant farms grew by almost thirteen percent. In the cotton producing states west of Alabama, where the majority of cotton production was moving, tenant farms increased while farm ownership fell by a little more than fifteen percent.[29]

Then, in the late 1920s the cotton South was rocked by two cataclysmic events. The first occurred in 1927 when floodwaters began to pour over the levees that had been built to protect rich croplands. It began raining in April and by the time it ended the Mississippi River "formed a vast yellow sea over one-thousand miles of land, and in places fifty miles wide."[30] These raging floodwaters covered thirteen percent of the state of Arkansas. William Faulkner describes the flood in a fictional account called "Old Man," in which groups of prisoners are brought from the Mississippi State Penitentiary to help rebuild the levees. The narrator of the story observes,

> Now there was water on both sides of the road and now, as if once they had become aware of movement in the water seemed to have given overdeception and concealment, they seemed to be able to watch it rising up the flanks of the dump; trees which a few miles back had stood on tall trunks above water now seemed to burst from the surface at the level of the lower branches like decorative shrubs on barbered lawns. The truck passed a Negro

> cabin. The water was up to window ledges. A women clutching two children squatted on the ridgepole, a man and a half grown youth, standing waist-deep, were hoisting a squealing pig onto the slanting roof of a barn, on the ridgepole of which sat a row of chickens and a turkey . . . then the road vanished.[31]

The flood of 1927 devastated much of the Arkansas and Mississippi delta. Three quarters of a million people were driven from their homes. Granville Whittiker of Edmonson, Arkansas remembered that the flood had been so bad that he and his father had been forced to sleep on a raft they made when they attempted to save some of their belongings.[32] Property damage from the flood was $220 million dollars area wide, with $14,936,000 damage in the Arkansas delta.[33] The damage was so severe that one eyewitness stated, "Whole towns were swept away; plantations became lakes; cattle and stock were lost by thousands."[34]

Southern farmers were still cleaning up from the devastating floodwaters when the stock market crashed in 1929. The depression affected farmers in a number of ways. As banks collapsed farmers had trouble getting credit, and without credit many farmers had trouble paying mortgages. Cotton prices plummeted sixty-one percent between September 1929 and September 1932, and in 1933 cotton reached an all-time low of five cents per pound.[35]

Both the bank collapse and drop in cotton prices made paying debts and mortgages almost impossible. The federal government did little to alleviate the suffering of farmers. Herbert Hoover's administration revolted against any idea of crop and price reductions to alleviate the suffering.[36] Hoover believed local communities should help one another, and if that was not enough they should turn to organizations like the Red Cross.[37] Farm owners and tenants thus stood on the brink of disaster when Franklin D. Roosevelt assumed the presidency in 1933.[38]

In the face of this economic devastation, landowners began evicting tenants and sharecroppers en masse. The decrease of tenant farms from 1930–1940 was astounding. From 1930–1940, tenant farms fell by nineteen percent for the entire South. [Table 4] In the same period, sharecropper and tenant farms in counties that would have STFU locals decreased by almost

TABLE 5. COTTON PRICE PER POUND, 1919–1935

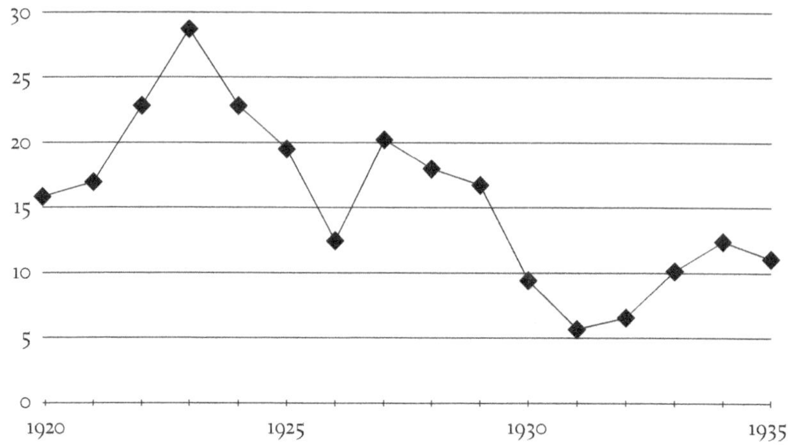

Source: Statistical History of the United States from Colonial Times to the Present

twenty-eight percent. In rough terms this equaled about ninety thousand people for the counties with STFU locals.[39] Historians attribute this decline to four factors. First, the world market for cotton was becoming increasingly competitive. International competition grew through the 1920s to the extent that in 1933–34, foreign sources produced and sold more cotton than United States cotton growers. This led many farmers to finally begin thinking about growing crops that were more profitable.[40] As farmers began to experiment with other crops many of them began to dismiss their tenants.

TABLE 6. DECREASE IN TENANT FARMS, 1930–1950

	30–35	35–40	40–45	45–50	30–40	40–50	30–50
South	13.58	6.36	19.60	22.31	19.07	37.53	49.44
West of Al.	.029	21.52	25.81	25.01	27.46	44.37	56.35
STFU Counties	8.31	21.23	11.76	16.67	27.77	26.44	46.87

Source: Fifteenth through the Seventeenth Census

Landowners also looked for ways to cut their overhead. The attempt to keep sharecroppers and tenant farmers on a plantation cost landowners much of their capital. In an economic downturn, it made financial sense for them to look for a way to cut overhead. Historians have found that more and more landowners were beginning to replace sharecroppers and tenant farmers with tractors and day laborers. The mechanization of cotton production would explode in the post-World War II period, but even in the 1930s many landowners began experimenting with tractors. Table 7 shows the astounding increase of tractors in counties with STFU locals. If we compare those to the southern states west of Alabama we see that that the counties that would have STFU locals experienced dramatic growth of tractors, which replaced many tenant farmers and sharecroppers. These early tractors were mostly "all-purpose" machines that performed many different tasks. They allowed the landowner to work larger areas of land himself and eliminate costs that he traditionally incurred in providing furnishes for sharecroppers and tenant farmers. But these early tractors were not equipped to pick cotton. Therefore many sharecroppers and tenant farmers who were displaced by tractors would still be needed to work as day laborers during cotton picking time.[41]

TABLE 7. PERCENTAGE GROWTH OF TRACTORS, 1930–1950

	1930–1940	1940–1950	1930–1950
United States	67.93	119.68	268.91
West of Alabama	118.39	176.87	504.65
STFU Counties	182.63	340.59	1145.26

Source: Fifteenth through the Seventeenth Census

In taking much of the cotton land out of production the Agricultural Adjustment Administration (AAA) helped create the third reason for the decrease in sharecroppers and tenant farmers. Although AAA contracts prohibited owners from evicting their tenant farmers and sharecroppers, some still used this opportunity to rid themselves of the financially burdensome redundant employees. The vast majority of owners no longer needed as many sharecroppers and tenant farmers to farm less land, so they simply dismissed their tenants.[42]

Franklin D. Roosevelt realized that "bold, persistent experimentation"[43] had to be used to fix the economy and restore farmers to their land. Immediately after his inauguration, the Roosevelt administration in conjunction with Congress began to experiment with solutions for the crisis that agriculture had been facing since the mid-1920s. On May 12, 1933, the President signed the Agricultural Adjustment Act into law. This act created the Agricultural Adjustment Administration (AAA) whose main purpose was to "increase the purchasing power of . . . farmers."[44] The AAA was charged with eliminating the surplus of certain crops, including cotton, in hope of bringing production of these crops in line with worldwide demand at a price that would bring farmers' purchasing power to World War I rates.[45] Cotton farmers already had large crops in the field by the time the act was passed. To offset a huge decline in cotton prices because of a surplus crop, the AAA paid farmers to plow up every third row of their cotton. In return for the plow-up the AAA paid farmers on average about eleven dollars per acre for 1933.[46]

Many landowners accepted the AAA payment plan because it gave them immediate access to cash, something most of them had not had for some time. But tenants and sharecroppers did not qualify for direct aid under the AAA. Many of the landowners had their tenant farmers and sharecroppers plow up their cotton, and then took the government money as their own. Under the ambiguous Section 7(a) of the AAA contract, the producer was required to "endeavor in good faith to bring the reduction of acreage contemplated in this contract in such a manner as to cause the least possible amount labor, economic and social disturbance. . . ."[47] Because the law put the landowner in charge of distributing AAA money, many landowners were able to double dip: they received the government's money for the plow-up of their tenant and sharecroppers' land, plus the money they could make from selling the remaining crops. Because they ended the year without a crop, many tenants found themselves on the side of the road without money, home or food.

Under the influence of landowners like Representative Joe Robinson of Arkansas, the administration relied upon the "good faith" of landowners to reduce their cotton production without abusing tenant farmers and sharecroppers. When Howard Kester, a Christian Socialist who would later be one of the STFU's national spokespersons, saw section 7(a) of the AAA contracts he called the Act an "economic monstrosity and bastard child of a decadent capitalism and a youthful Fascism."[48] Section 7(a) did not work, and by the summer of 1934 thousands of sharecroppers and tenant farmers were forced off the land that they had worked for many years.[49]

From the 1860s to the 1930s the South experienced massive upheaval as the old plantation system changed or withered away. From a Civil War that devastated the agricultural economy, to a political battle over who would control the land, to devastatingly low cotton prices, to war-time prosperity, to post war collapse of cotton prices, to floods, and the Great Depression, the road from plantations to large scale agribusiness enterprises moved with dizzying speed that left most sharecroppers and tenant farmers wondering what had happened. In the seventy years after the Civil War, sharecroppers and tenant farmers found themselves at the bottom of society. Like most southerners, they had been taught from childhood that to own a piece of land, to work that land, and to support a family was the duty of every man. But reality has a way of grinding ideals into dust. In the midst of massive economic and personal upheavals a group of white and black sharecroppers and tenant farmers who had recently been evicted from their homes on the Norcross Plantation, met at the Sunnyside school in St. Francis County, Arkansas, to found the Southern Tenant Farmers' Union. These men saw the changes all around them and realized they had to do something to protect their way of life and to feed their families. But why Arkansas? Why not Texas, Mississippi, or Georgia? In the end it would come down to local factors in Marked Tree, Arkansas. In Marked Tree, despair, hopelessness, and fear gripped the minds of sharecroppers and tenant farmers as their way of life was dying. Into this chaos arose local leaders who would try, with little success, to halt the change and to restore a way of life that had dominated the South for seventy years.

CHAPTER TWO

ON A HOT, STEAMY JULY NIGHT IN 1934, Burt Williamson, the son of a nineteenth-century Ku Klux Klan leader, and Isaac Shaw, the son of a slave, sat face to face in a small one-room schoolhouse on the edge of the Fairview Plantation in Poinsett County, Arkansas. These two aging men from fundamentally different worlds were meeting with two socialists and sixteen other sharecroppers and tenant farmers to create the Southern Tenant Farmers' Union.

Many others have told the story of the STFU.[1] It seems so simple: a group of sharecroppers, black and white, put aside their lifelong racial anxieties and founded an integrated union that organized tens of thousands of sharecroppers and tenant farmers in seven southern states. In this typical narrative, the union arose from decidedly indigenous groups; there were no outside agitators.[2] In many ways, this story has become the accepted narrative of the Southern Tenant Farmers' Union, but the reality was never that simple.

In the 1960s and 1970s, H. L. Mitchell, one of the socialists at that first meeting, loved going around the country and telling the moving story of this small group of white and black men founding the union with little or no help. His adventure in myth making simplified a very complex story that began in the spring of 1933 and culminated in the July 1934 meeting at the Fairview Schoolhouse. Many different actors were involved in the founding of the union. Socialists like Norman Thomas, William Amberson, Clay East, H. L. Mitchell, and Claude Waldren worked with local figures such as Alvin Nunnaly, Isaac Shaw, Burt Williamson, Brit McKinney, and the masses of nameless sharecroppers and tenant farmers. Each actor came with different agendas. Diversity of personalities, agendas, and tactics characterized the people at the beginning of the union, and is key to understanding the STFU. This diversity would shape the union's founding, life, and death.

In many ways, the STFU's story was that of forgotten men and women who sacrificed their ways of life and fought for basic human rights. But to ignore leaders such as H. L. Mitchell would be to distort the story's complexity. Mitchell towers over the memory of the union because he worked for most of his life to preserve its history. More importantly, he was actively involved in fighting for what he perceived to be sharecroppers and tenant farmers' rights. Mitchell was not an easily understood man. For the most part, this complex man has been made into a caricature: simple farm boy discovers socialism and spends the rest of his life struggling to create some form of social justice in America. Mitchell liked to tell this story. To understand completely the union's founding, the extraordinary lives of H. L. Mitchell and Henry Clay East must be unraveled from mythology. Mitchell made this task more difficult by being a consummate salesman who constantly recreated his life story. He seemed to have a clear understanding of his life's historical significance and wrote a number of biographies to guide historians in their quest to write his story. Reading the many life histories that he left, the earliest dating from 1936 and the latest from 1979, strikes one with how much his story changed in significant ways over time.[3] He loved for audiences of young radicals to see him as the hero of the STFU. In many ways he was heroic, but no one is always heroic. When H. L. Mitchell is extricated from the mythology he helped create, a much more complex and nuanced man emerges.

Henry Leland Mitchell was born in 1906 in Halls, Tennessee, a tiny farming community located sixty miles north of Memphis. The world into which Mitchell was born was one of diminishing expectations. He was always fond of saying that his family had descended the agricultural ladder. Mitchell's grandfather, James A. Mitchell, fought in the Confederate army and after the war, James Mitchell became a harness maker and itinerate Baptist preacher. After relocating in Waldron, Arkansas, on the western edge of the state, Mitchell's grandfather prospered. With his newfound wealth he returned to Tennessee and purchased a large farm near Brownsville on the Hatchie River. By 1906, Mitchell's grandfather had returned to Halls and was living on a small farm about a mile north of town.[4]

Mitchell's father, James Young Mitchell, never became a landowner. He was a successful tenant farmer most of his early life, owning his own team of animals and farming tools. He worked for a brief time in a mill and traveled the countryside as a Baptist preacher. By the time H. L. Mitchell was a young man, his father had moved to town and was operating a barbershop.[5]

As with most southerners of his time, land, race, and religion defined H. L. Mitchell's life. Mitchell worked on the land from the age of eight, "picking cotton in fall, strawberries in spring, and then chopping or weeding cotton in summer."[6] It was in these strawberry fields that Mitchell would meet Johnnie, his first childhood friend. Johnnie's skin color just happened to be darker than Mitchell's. They ran all over the countryside playing like any friends would. One night Mitchell decided to invite Johnnie to spend the night with him. They were only six years old, but Mitchell was told a black boy could not stay in their house. Thirty years later, Mitchell still could not make any sense of this event.[7]

This would not be Mitchell's only experience with the South's racial code. Five years later, during World War I, Mitchell witnessed a lynching. Mitchell's memories of the event were still vivid in the 1960s and 1970s. The angry crowd tied the man to an iron post surrounded by wood crates and wood shavings, saturated in kerosene or gasoline. The victim began crying "Oh God, is there no help for a widow's son?" Then someone lit the fire. Mitchell reported that he ran away from the scene as quickly as he could in utter disgust.[8]

These events and probably others throughout his life would haunt Mitchell. On one hand, these experiences horrified him and caused him to rebel against the rigid code of racial conduct all whites were expected to follow. Nevertheless, he was still a man of his time, and race would plague him and the STFU.

In 1919, when Mitchell was thirteen, he and his family moved to Ruleville, Mississippi. Mitchell's father ran a barbershop, and it was here that Mitchell made his first sharecrop. In Ruleville, the family seemed to prosper, but a tornado destroyed their prosperity in 1920, forcing them out of Mississippi to the small town of Moscow, Tennessee.[9]

Moscow would prove to be a major crossroad of Mitchell's life. During the presidential campaign of 1920, Mitchell heard his first speech by a Socialist Party member. The speaker that day was the local "horse doctor," John Morris. Later in life, Mitchell would claim that he sought out Morris, and that the older man completed his conversion to socialism. Mitchell claimed that Morris provided him with "Little Blue Books" by authors such as Upton Sinclair and Karl Marx. "Little Blue Books," first published by E. Haldeman-Julius in Girard, Kansas, consisted of an eclectic collection of simplistic writings on a plethora of topics: there were mystery books, classics, ancient writings, how-to books, and most importantly pro-evolution and socialist classics.[10] This account of a sudden conversion in 1920 does not match earlier memories. Mitchell's shift to socialism and atheism actually arose out of a lifetime's experience.

Like race, religion was at the center of Mitchell's early life. Later in life Mitchell would profess atheism, but he was not born an atheist. Mitchell described his early beliefs as "fundamentalist," and in fact he had grown up in a preacher's family.[11] Both Mitchell's grandfather and father were Baptist preachers. Mitchell remembered he went to the Baptist church every Sunday and Wednesday and to the Methodist Church on Tuesday for prayer meetings.

His mother seems to have been one very important formative source of Mitchell's drift from religion. She had married young and was forced to move in with Mitchell's grandfather. "Brother Mitchell," as his grandfather was called, would have many preachers stay at his home, and Mitchell's mother was expected to work for them. Against her will she cooked and cleaned for them and even did their laundry. She was a strong-willed person who did not understand why she was forced to serve these able bodied men. She slowly built up a strong sense of resentment towards preachers and organized religion that she passed on to her son. She told her son that most preachers were hypocrites, and he seems to have taken her advice to heart.[12]

When her own husband felt called to the ministry, Mrs. Mitchell must have felt great apprehension. For months on end, Mitchell's father would leave the family alone while he tended to the "Lord's Work." He had promised to come back with money, but he always came back broke. Soon it became painfully obvious that many of these divine calls involved other women. Around the end of World War I, Mitchell's father was caught with another man's wife. The church that had ordained him held a trial and revoked his ministerial license. The family was shamed; Mitchell's father left the ministry and the farm and became a barber. For Mitchell, religion began to lose its plausibility. While his mother worked on the farm and remained faithful to her preacher husband, he had been gallivanting around the country wasting their money and sleeping with other women.[13]

Another phase in his religious evolution occurred in 1925 during the Scopes trial. Mitchell's later account that he had returned to Halls an atheist in 1923 does not match earlier evidence.[14] As a fundamentalist, Mitchell was opposed to the idea that humans descended from monkeys.[15] He considered creationist presidential candidate William Jennings Bryan "the greatest living man on earth."[16] Then one day Mitchell was looking at the local newspaper and came across an advertisement that said, "To oppose evolution you should know what it is." This intrigued him and he ordered his first of many "Blue Books" from Girard, Kansas.[17] Over the next few months, Mitchell would find the ideas of atheism and socialism presented in these books to have a ring of truth.

By 1927, Mitchell had begun to give up two essential features of his South: white supremacy and fundamentalist religion. Mitchell would always wrestle with race. He was a child of the South and would always have a paternalistic view of black southerners. When he gave up on fundamentalist Christianity, he merely switched faiths. His version of socialism was as dogmatic and absolute as any fundamentalist preacher's view of Christianity. Historians have argued that H. L. Mitchell was an aberration in the South. In many ways he was, but he was still a product of his time.

Mitchell lived in Halls until 1927 while his family was already living in Tyronza, Arkansas. Mitchell's father was running a barbershop that was doing well, and he wrote Mitchell asking him to come to Tyronza where "Land is rich and one can make two bales of cotton to the acre." With great excitement Mitchell went to Arkansas to see this "Land of Milk and Honey" for himself.[18]

Mitchell had been offered work on the Brackenseik Plantation that was located about four miles north of Tyronza. The Brackenseik brothers had offered Mitchell land plus a part time job as the company store's clerk.

When he arrived at the plantation, what Mitchell saw troubled him. The cabins were dilapidated and dangerous for human habitation. Located down muddy back roads that were impassable by car, Mitchell discovered that sharecropper houses had been made with green lumber that had caused doors to sag and walls to buckle. He also found that light was coming into the shacks thorough huge cracks in the floors, walls, and ceilings. Mitchell was sickened by what he saw, and he quickly decided to return to Tennessee.[19] This experience would have ended Mitchell's life in Arkansas had his father not convinced him to take over a pressing shop, which was located in the back of his barbershop. Mitchell, with no experience or training in the pressing business, decided to take his father up on this offer, and moved to Arkansas.[20]

In 1927, Mitchell moved into a three-room house in the sleepy plantation town of Tyronza. He bought a Model T Ford and renovated it into a side-panel truck. After painting a sign on his truck that read "Tyronza Cleaners, H. L. Mitchell, Prop.," Mitchell set out on the back roads of Poinsett County. Day in and day out Mitchell called on plantation owners and riding bosses attempting to convince them to have their clothes pressed at his shop. By late 1927, Mitchell had a thriving business, had moved to a new location at the end of Main Street, and was on his way to a respectable life in the tiny cotton town.[21]

As Mitchell settled into his new life, he became acquainted with his neighbors. His next-door neighbor was a "tough, stocky, and outspoken" man named Clay East.[22] The East family was an old established family in eastern Arkansas. Clay East's grandfather migrated from Tennessee to become one of the first settlers in Eastern Arkansas. His father owned a successful grocery store and large farm.[23] His uncle, Alex East, was a successful landowner who, in April 1927, had a two-hundred acre cotton farm that would have produced a large crop had the great Mississippi River flood of that year not destroyed it.[24] Clay East was several years older than Mitchell. He had attended Blue Mountain Academy, a Southern Baptist school in northern Mississippi, for one year before attending the Gulf Coast Military School in Mississippi. After graduating, East received orders to report to Officers' Training School, but World War I ended before he arrived. East returned to Tyronza where he worked on the family farm. He eventually bought a gas station; one of three in town, and by 1927 was comfortably successful.[25]

Mitchell did not move to Tyronza to spread socialism or begin a union. He came to make money and take care of his family. In the two years from Mitchell's move to Tyronza to the Stock Market crash in October 1929, socialism for Mitchell and East remained an intellectual enterprise. They would spend hours discussing the subject. At first East found socialism offensive and rejected it. But, like so many Americans, the crash changed the way he looked at socialism. After the crash, East began to lose business, and he wondered how he was going to make it. One day, East came into Mitchell's office with an idea to help his business. He wanted the three gas stations in town to take turns being open so that each owner could make a profit and stay in business. Mitchell laughed and said that this was a good idea, but it sounded a lot like socialism. East protested that this was just common sense, but Mitchell sent East home with Little Blue Books to read. One of these books would convince East that socialism was the only answer to his and the nation's woes.[26]

Upton Sinclair's *Letters To Judd* were fictional letters that Sinclair wrote to a carpenter. In these letters, Sinclair explained why capitalism as a system was destined to crumble and why only the answers offered by the Socialist Party could help the common man. East was convinced and began to order other Blue Books. He also subscribed to Oscar Ameringer's militantly socialist newspaper, *The American Guardian*. Mitchell and East began to speak to anyone who came into their shops about socialism, and by 1930, their end of Main Street was known as "Red Square."[27]

Mitchell and East talked about socialism until sometime in 1932 when they heard that socialist leader and perennial presidential candidate Norman Thomas was going to be in Memphis. They decided to drive to Memphis to hear him speak. At the Ellis Auditorium in Memphis, four or five thousand others gathered to hear the speech. When they arrived back in Arkansas, Mitchell and East were excited and began to talk about forming a socialist local in Tyronza.[28]

The Socialist Party required a minimum of seven members to form a local chapter. Mitchell and East had no trouble convincing their wives to join, and soon a sharecropper named Alvin Nunnally and his wife plus a local carpenter, whose name Mitchell had forgotten, also joined. Immediately Mitchell faced a problem: East had second thoughts. East had political ambitions and planned to run for town constable. He intended to run as a Democrat and knew that being a socialist would hurt his chances. After winning the election, East eagerly joined the socialist local in Tyronza and promised to protect it from repression by townspeople; however, Mitchell had his first of many doubts about East's reliability.[29]

All over the world in the midst of the Depression people in all walks of life seriously examined radical political options. In May 1933, Clarence Senior, the National Secretary of the Socialist Party of America, wanted to call a "Continental Congress" to draft a program to take to the President and to the Congress. Almost 4,000 delegates responded to the call, including two young men from Tyronza.[30]

Mitchell and East had been selected to attend the congress in Washington by the Tyronza socialist local and went to a Socialist Party pre-congress planning meeting in Memphis. This Memphis meeting would be momentous in many ways. It would be at this meeting that East and Mitchell would meet J. C. Thompson, a 70-year-old socialist who had been involved in the camp meeting days of American socialism. Thompson energized East and Mitchell with tales of radicalism in Texas, Oklahoma, Arkansas, and Louisiana in the early days of the century and made the two young men dream of tapping into the spirit of that old revolutionary movement. They also met William Amberson, a local Memphis socialist who became an essential connection between the Socialist Party and the STFU.[31]

At the Memphis meeting, Clay East also started along the path of disillusionment with the Socialist Party's factionalism. The Memphis local had the same splits that were beginning to plague the national Party. When Norman Thomas began his rise to prominence in the Party during the 1920s, he moved the Party away from the dream of building a simple working-class socialism and towards a socialism that included workers, farmers, and middle-class progressives. Thomas wanted to build liberal coalitions that would prove viable in national and state elections. By 1933, three factions had developed in the Socialist Party.[32] The two larger factions were the Old Guard and the Progressives. The Old Guard was composed largely, but not exclusively, of middle-aged or elderly members who had been in the Party since the early days. They were strong in New York, Pennsylvania and Connecticut and had large numbers in the older trade unions. They controlled the Socialist Party journal, *The New Leader*. The Progressives were newer members attracted to Thomas's common-sense socialism and Clarence Senior's youthful exuberance. They tended to reject dogmatic Marxist formulations. Their goal was the realignment of American politics so that there would be a party that would represent labor and dirt farmers. A much smaller but vocal group comprised the Militants. Philosophically they were more attracted to Lenin's views of revolution in contrast to the Old Guard's social democracy. The Militants tended to oppose the rigid discipline of the Communist Party's Third International and to be critical of the Soviet Union's denial of civil liberties, but they were enthusiastic about the Russian economy. Norman Thomas was a Progressive but knew how to court the Militants. This national party factionalism would explode in 1936, but at the local level, as the Memphis meeting made clear, it was already becoming a problem.[33] The Old Guard union leadership in Memphis alienated East, who was closest to the Progressives. This factionalism caused East to back out of going to the Congress in Washington. In May 1933, H. L. Mitchell, then 27-years-old, set out alone on his first of many trips to Washington, D.C.[34]

Looking back on this event, Mitchell was convinced that the Continental Congress was the "nearest thing ever seen in America to the First All Union Congress of Soviets in Moscow, when the Bolsheviks launched the Communist Revolution."[35] Later in life, Mitchell remembered the militancy of the 1933 Congress. He recalled a fiery speech made by John A. Simpson, then president of the National Farmers Union, who called on delegates to take over the United States government on behalf of workers and farmers.[36] This conference radicalized Mitchell and placed him on the Socialist Party's left wing in 1934. Whereas East was a Progressive, Mitchell, in 1933, became a Militant.

Socialists in Girard, Kansas, greatly influenced H. L. Mitchell's intellectual and political development. J. A. Wayland had been a Republican businessman who converted to socialism in the late nineteenth century. After a number of failed enterprises, he moved to the small coal-mining town of Girard, Kansas. Here, Wayland preached his brand of socialism (which blended Edward Bellamy's utopian visions with Lawrence Grounland's so-called scientific socialism) in a newspaper called *The Appeal to Reason*. Wayland's socialism, with its vision of a better world guaranteed by the iron laws of history attracted a large number of poor farmers and working people in the southwest. This message was kept alive into the 1930s through newspapers like the *Haldeman-Julius Weekly* and *American Guardian* and through the Little Blue Books.[37] These later newspapers indoctrinated Mitchell in the message of the socialist movement's left wing. It is interesting that in socialist Martha Johnson's first letter to Norman Thomas about Mitchell she stated that he was a "reading fool" who kept current issues of these newspapers plus "some communist literature" in his store.[38] In September 1936, remembering back to 1934, Mitchell claimed "In the beginning I was perhaps more a communist than a socialist, but I knew if I tied up with the former openly we would never have a chance to do anything." In 1964, Mitchell denied vehemently that he had meant what he said. The only argument he could give in 1964 to prove that he was not closer to the communists was that those charges might "ruin a man's career, especially here in the South." But the contemporary evidence suggests that in 1933–34 he held to a radical dogmatic version of socialism that was closer to the Communist Party.[39]

The Socialist Party's Militant wing, made up of idealistic and energetic young people, was in many ways closer to the Communist Party of the 1930s. To understand how Mitchell thought in the STFU's early days it is important to understand the communist ideology of the "Third Period." At the Sixth Congress of the Communist International in 1928, delegates decreed that capitalism had gone through three periods since the World War. In the first period, the post-war crisis had led to the beginning of the revolutionary workers' movement centered in the Communist Party. When the first epoch ended in 1923, the Comintern declared that the world economy had moved into a period of economic growth, which had forced the communist movement on the defensive. A third period began in 1928. A crisis within capitalism had begun, they argued, due to "rapid technological expansion" and the incapacity of markets to respond to this growth. This, the Communist International believed, would lead to a new crisis and renewed militancy by the working class. In practice, this meant a more "militant" Communist Party. Electoral politics were no longer important. The Communist Party ran candidates in only a few cities, and many members argued against any political activity. Militant action was all that counted. The working classes, so they thought, needed the revolutionary leadership of the Communist Party to move them through the class struggle to the ultimate victory of a Soviet America. In this "Third Period" the Communist Party was involved in unemployment and hunger demonstrations and, most importantly, in dual unionism. It formed the Trade Union Unity League that supported three main unions: National Textile Workers Industrial Union, National Miners Union, and the Needle Trade Workers Industrial Union. The chief task of these new unions was to fight against the "social fascism" of the American Federation of Labor.

In the realm of ideology, Third Period communists believed that because the structural collapse of American capitalism was so severe there could never be a recovery. It followed in their minds that there would soon be a great and inevitable conflict between the working class and the fascist forces of capitalism. This was an extremely dogmatic time in the history of the American Communist Party; factions were prohibited and no internal dissention was allowed in the Party press.[40]

The Socialist Party in some ways agreed with the Communist Party. Socialists believed that capitalism had reached a crisis in 1929. They believed that workers were the key to improving society, although Norman Thomas and other Progressive socialists made it clear that they must have the help of middle-class men and women as well. Many Old Guard and Progressive socialists believed that the crisis of capitalism had to be stopped or it would lead to the breakdown of the "politico-economic" system, which would lead to catastrophe and social anarchy. Old Guard and Progressive socialists also accepted the class struggle between capitalists and workers but absolutely rejected the view of the class struggle that saw it as a "mystic act of salvation by faith, which almost absolves them from hard and intelligent work to organize labor economically or politically." While Third Period communists rejected democracy as a form of social fascism, Old Guard and Progressive socialists thought that the new world could only come through the democratic institutions that then existed: trade unions and political parties. Equally important was the Socialist stress on non-dogmatic leadership that allowed for real Party disagreements on theory and action that could be discussed in the Party press. Communists had rejected factionalism in 1928 and would not allow any vocal disagreements in the Party press.[41]

The Socialist Party's Militant wing, into which Mitchell fit most comfortably, consisted of a small group of men and women eager to move the Socialist Party to the left. The Militants were the most vocal socialists who wanted to see their party and the Communist Party work together. While most Militants rejected the dogmatic communist leadership style, they did like the Communist Party's analysis of the future and its evolutionary faith in the inevitable revolution. This was Mitchell's ideology in 1933 and 1934.

Even after the Union's founding, Mitchell was still enthralled with the Communist Party's ideological understanding of the Depression. In August 1934, Amberson reported to Thomas that Mitchell was not out organizing locals because he believed the revolution was just around the corner. Thomas was concerned enough about this to write Mitchell and remind him that the revolution "is not coming tomorrow or next month or even next year. Our job is to build sound organization and to educate the members of the organization." In 1970, East wrote to remind Mitchell that he had been the more radical of the two, even refusing to pick up hitchhikers because "it makes them class conscious."[42] Although Mitchell would hate the communists by 1937–1939, in 1933–1934 his reading of southwestern socialists had made the left-wing analysis plausible. Mitchell shared with the communists a utopian vision of a coming revolution that was absolutely certain, as certain as the coming of the kingdom of God for fundamentalist Christians. Mitchell quickly learned to temper his position to get support from Norman Thomas and the Socialist Party. He would also lose faith in this radicalism as he began to interact with the Communist Party in 1937. Like so many others, Mitchell would come to question the dogmatic communist leadership style and the inevitability of the revolution.[43]

At the Continental Congress that so excited Mitchell, the 4,000 delegates passed a resolution that built upon the original Declaration of Independence's claim that the people could "alter or abolish" the government. Affirming this first Declaration, delegates called on workers and farmers to band together and build a new society based on a "new economic system of justice and freedom."[44]

After returning to Tyronza, Mitchell settled back into his business and talked to anyone who would listen about the coming revolution. In late 1933, the Civil Works Administration (CWA) came to Tyronza, and many tenant farmers and sharecroppers believed that the local planters who controlled the job assignments were giving jobs only to their favorite sharecroppers and tenant farmers. By this time Mitchell had a favorable reputation among the sharecroppers and tenant farmers of Tyronza, and one day a group of men came to see him at his pressing shop. They asked Mitchell to go to Harrisburg, Arkansas and demand that the CWA give work to all the people who wanted jobs. Mitchell refused to go with a mob of men to the county seat but persuaded them to form the Tyronza Unemployment League. Unemployment Leagues had been popping up all over the nation. Originally, the Communist Party had formed them in August 1931, and this seems to be yet more evidence that Mitchell, while not a member of the Communist Party, was at least influenced by it.[45]

The first act of the Tyronza Unemployment League was to call for a mass meeting in Tyronza with CWA leaders. According to Mitchell, five hundred men and women turned out for the meeting. After voting on the league's bylaws and constitution, Poinsett County's emergency relief director, Mrs. Alex East, arrived to discuss what needed to be done to alleviate the complaints. She asked to address the crowd and called on all those present to join her in reciting the "Pledge of Allegiance" to prove that they were "good Americans." Although her motivation is unclear, it is safe to assume that she and the others in the Poinsett County's ruling class honestly wanted to know if the mob of people consisted of genuine Americans or, as some of them probably suspected, of communists. According to Mitchell, Mrs. East began the pledge and almost immediately she was interrupted by a sharecropper who shouted, "That Boy Scout oath is alright, I guess, but this is not the time or place—every man here tonight came to see about getting one of those relief jobs. If you have anything to tell us about the jobs, let's hear it. Otherwise, you sit down and let somebody who does have something to tell us that we want to hear." According to Mitchell, the relief director "slunk into her seat . . . just like a whuped cur dog." After this embarrassing outburst, the state relief director spoke and promised that all who had attended the meeting would be hired the next day.[46]

The Tyronza Unemployment League only lasted for a couple more months. The sharecroppers and tenant farmers had received what they wanted—jobs. However, for Mitchell, the success of the league re-energized him and sent him out into the back roads to try to tap into that old-time Arkansas radicalism that he had heard about from J. C. Thompson.[47]

Radical political movements were not new to Arkansas. Although the Democratic Party continued to dominate the state and some supported the Republican Party, many small farmers thought neither party represented their economic interests. As early as 1880, the Arkansas Greenback Party, with its core membership drawn from disgruntled workers and small farmers, ran a slate of candidates to replace the gold standard with greenbacks. The Party won twenty-seven percent of the vote in the gubernatorial race, which suggested that many Arkansans were not satisfied with the hard money politics of the Democratic Party, which they felt helped large planters and industrialists. By 1886, the Agricultural Wheel had entered state politics with an attack on monopolies and attempts to establish cooperative stores. The organization frightened the Democratic Party enough that it adopted the platform of the Wheel and won the election. In 1888, the Wheel and the Knights of Labor joined to form the Union Labor Party. This group also called for a new monetary system based on soft money and regulation of corporations. In the 1888 election, the Party received forty-six percent of the vote in the gubernatorial race. By the time the Populists organized in the state, Democrats had taken a new agrarian stand that weakened opposition to their control. However, some Arkansans were still not satisfied.[48]

Local socialists formed the Arkansas Socialist Party in 1902. It quickly grew into a significant political party in the state's northwest and central regions among townspeople, coal miners, and farmers. The Party, like so many southwestern Socialist Party locals, utilized newspapers, pamphlets, and camp meetings to spread its message. These camp meetings had all the flair of an evangelical revival and would last for days. They boasted big named speakers such Eugene V. Debs, Oscar Ameringer, and Mother

Jones. But the most important way that socialism spread was on the lips of local men like J. C. Thompson and Sam Faubus.[49]

J. C. Thompson, who would be instrumental in lighting a fire under Mitchell and East, lived in Texarkana, Arkansas and became an avid promoter of socialism in Arkansas and other southwestern states. He traveled from town to town to make sure that the locals were working hard for socialism. He preached evangelical-like sermons, calling workers and farmers to see their plight and to join the Socialist Party to end oppression. Thompson and others did not speak in high sounding words or about difficult Marxist theory. The southwest socialists were far closer to the old Farmer's Alliance and the Populists. These speakers rooted their message in the daily hardships of common people they spoke to and offered simple answers: a revolution was coming; no matter what capitalists did they could not stop the progress of history.[50]

The rank and file usually came to the Party through reading and hearing speeches and debates. Sam Faubus was the head of the socialist local in Greasy Creek, Arkansas, located in Madison County. Like so many others, he came to socialism through reading newspapers published in Girard, Kansas and attending speeches and socialist camp meetings. By the 1930s, he and his son Orval were holding debates in the local area to win converts. In this way socialism spread through Arkansas and attracted many adherents.[51]

After the publication of historian Arthur M. Schlesinger Jr's book, *The Coming of the New Deal,* Mitchell wrote Schlesinger trying to correct what he thought were mistakes in the book. Mitchell told Schlesinger that he and East had been "floundering about" until November 1933 when two of the oldest and most effective organizers for the Socialist Party came to Arkansas. Eddie and Martha Johnson had come to help Mitchell and East gain new members for the Arkansas Socialist Party. The Tyronza local had found out that Norman Thomas was going to be in Nashville, Tennessee, on February 16, 1934, giving a lecture entitled "The Aims of Socialism" to the local chapter of the League for Industrial Democracy. Thomas had long been interested in sharecroppers and tenant farmers, and the Johnsons thought that this would be the time for Thomas to see the plantation system's horrors. So they sat down to write him a letter. The Johnsons' letter shows that their main concern was getting votes for Thomas in the 1934 election. Nevertheless, they also informed Thomas that in the Arkansas delta he would find "the true proletariat." Although these sharecroppers and tenant farmers might be inarticulate, the Johnsons believed they were "moving irresistibly toward revolution." According to the Johnsons, the center of this revolutionary spirit was Tyronza, Arkansas. They wanted Thomas to come to the area because they feared that the Communists would discover these people and organize them, or that armed sharecroppers and tenant farmers would take matters into their own hands. At the top of this letter Thomas wrote, "I consider this Important." In response, Thomas agreed to come to Tyronza for a full day's visit before a Memphis speech on February 17, 1934.[52]

Norman Thomas arrived in Memphis early on Saturday morning, February 17. Following breakfast with William Amberson and H. L. Mitchell, all three drove across the Mississippi River and on to Tyronza. Thomas planned to speak at the town's schoolhouse, but first he wanted to meet sharecroppers and tenant farmers and find out what their lives were really like. We do not know much about his visit with sharecroppers and tenant farmers. We know of at least two men whose families he visited: Clayton Taylor and Edward Boston. Both men and their families were later kicked off the land they farmed, and both believed their meeting with Thomas had been the cause.[53]

After lunch at Clay East's, Thomas prepared his speech. Early that afternoon about 500 people from all the little Poinsett County farming communities gathered in and around the Tyronza schoolhouse. About half of the people were sharecroppers and tenant farmers, and the other half were planters and middle-class townspeople. As men and women packed into the small auditorium, meant only to hold 200, they could not help noticing the two flags hanging on the wall behind the podium. On top was the American flag, but below it was another—the Red Flag, emblazoned in gold with the words "Socialist Local Tyronza."[54]

At 2:30 that afternoon Norman Thomas began his speech by stating that he had come to the Arkansas delta, "which is the rich treasure of God and nature, and found that men and women were living in shacks that you wouldn't put cows in." While he did not talk about it at the meeting, earlier in the day Thomas had visited the Fairview Plantation and seen a new cow barn with concrete floors.[55] The idea of giving cows concrete floors while humans lived in squalor had deeply offended Thomas. He was not finished with animal comparisons. He told the audience that he had seen a sign on the highway advertising bears at the St. Louis Zoo. "I tell you," he cried with passion, "a bear is in luck compared with a share-cropper." Thomas mused that he had seen the St. Louis Zoo and informed the crowd that the zookeepers did, in fact, take care of the bears because the bears were valuable. The crowd laughed, but many in the crowd understood his point: while bears in the zoo or cows in the barn were important, sharecroppers were not. Sharecroppers and tenant farmers' houses were dilapidated and run down; their diet was inadequate; their health was poor.

Thomas had little sympathy for landowners who argued that they suffered equally with their sharecroppers and tenant farmers. He challenged landowners to try to live the life their laborers were forced to live. Calling sharecroppers and tenant farmers "forgotten men," Thomas argued that government had irrationally reduced the cotton crop while sharecroppers and tenant farmers went without adequate clothing. The sight of a family he met that lived five miles from the closest school angered him. Thomas was horrified and stunned that sharecroppers and tenant farmers could be thrown off their farms without any warning. He informed the crowd that the situation in the Arkansas delta was worse than any in the cities or mining camps.

Thomas ended his speech with a parable. He invited the crowd to imagine itself shipwrecked on an uninhabited island. The island was very fertile, and in the settlement's early days tasks were portioned out to people based on their talents to meet the community's needs. Everyone worked for the community's benefit and not for themselves. Then one day the community found boxes of tools and machinery washed up on the beach. Thomas, in dramatic fashion, pointed to the men and women sitting on the front row and said that he and this small group had been the ones to find the tools. This group, Thomas suggested, was faced with two choices. First, they could call the community together and announce that tools and machinery had been found, and now, working together, the whole community could have all their material needs met. This, according to Thomas, was socialism. On the other hand, the group that had discovered the tools could organize the Robinson Crusoe Island Development Corporation. The new corporation would call the community together and tell it that the corporation would now own the land and tools. The land would be rented to individuals who would give a portion of their crop to the corporation. If the renter produced too much then there would be a forty percent reduction in crops. Thomas ended his speech by arguing that sharecroppers and tenant farmers were the "victims of a system" of capitalist inefficiency. The solution was to take the large farms and sell them to tenants who would work them collectively. Later that night in Memphis, Thomas repeated this speech. Thomas and the Arkansas Socialists had indeed begun to tap into the traditional radicalism of Arkansas, but it would be in ways that these socialists would never quite understand.[56]

The reaction to this speech was quite diverse depending on whether one was a socialist, planter, sharecropper, or government official. The publicity the Tyronza socialist movement received from Thomas's visit excited Mitchell and East. Because of the excitement and activity generated by the visit, Mitchell misunderstood a portion of Thomas's speech. Mitchell wrote to Eddie Johnson five days after Thomas's speech and said he did not agree with Thomas's plan to put sharecroppers and tenant farmers on individually owned farms. While Mitchell made it clear to Johnson that he was excited about Thomas' visit in general, he was concerned that Thomas would give in to bourgeois plans for individual ownership. When Thomas heard of Mitchell's misunderstanding, he quickly wrote to Mitchell and informed him that he had misunderstood the speech's thrust. Thomas restated that he wanted collectives that would not be as ruinous as the Russian experiment, which Thomas believed had moved too quickly to collectivize people who did not want or understand collectives.[57]

One of the most important local socialists to react to Thomas's speech was a socialist professor in Memphis. Their relationship is one of the forgotten stories in the history of the STFU. Over time, William Ruthrauff Amberson became a close and trusted advisor to Norman Thomas. Amberson was born in Harrisburg, Pennsylvania in 1894. He received his doctorate in biology from Princeton in 1922 and assumed his first teaching post in Physiology at Tennessee College of Medicine. He would stay in

Memphis until 1937, when he moved to the University of Maryland. By 1934, he was active in organizing the Memphis unemployed, surveying their identity and origins. Amberson was a Progressive within the Socialist Party who was not interested in a future revolution. He was instead a humanitarian who only wanted to alleviate the present suffering of people. Amberson quickly grew weary of Mitchell's radicalism. As late as 1939, he wanted to remove Mitchell from the union's leadership and replace him with a more moderate socialist[58]

In a letter written on February 22, 1934, Amberson offered Norman Thomas advice to keep him from making foolish mistakes that would give credence to the claims of planters and their allies that Thomas was an uninformed outsider meddling in things he did not understand. First, Amberson clarified that the 1933 AAA cotton reduction contract had, in fact, called on planters to split up their "plow up" money with their tenants. Thomas had criticized the government for not calling on the planters to be fair to tenants. Instead, Amberson called Thomas to a guarded and more moderate position: "I think we should distinguish between the intent of the government and what actually happens." Instead of attacking the entire planter class and the government, Amberson cautioned that the Socialist Party should instead attack the "chiseler, the planters who were ripping off their sharecroppers and tenant farmers." Secondly, Amberson tried to help Thomas learn the terminology of southern agriculture. Having spent his entire life in the North and in cities, Thomas continued to call sharecropping "crop-sharing." Amberson gently reminded Thomas that he might be more clearly understood if he were to use the regular terminology. Thomas was obviously not offended by the letter because from this time on Amberson would be a constant advisor to Thomas on issues that affected the Socialist Party and the South.[59]

Far less congenial was the planters and their newspaper allies' reaction. Two days after Thomas's speech, Mitchell wrote Thomas, "We have stirred up a hornet's nest down here in this section."[60] Although in later years actions of the STFU and Norman Thomas would be greeted with violence, the initial planter reaction consisted of a war of words. Days after Thomas's speeches the local papers began to attack him. The *Memphis Commercial Appeal*, in an editorial entitled "Erroneous," claimed that Thomas, in his short visit, had gained a faulty impression of Arkansas farming conditions. The planters and their allies tended to argue that every area of the world had its share of shiftless men and women who lived in poverty because they "lack . . . pride and industry."[61] In the *Memphis Press Scimitar* on Monday, February 19, 1934, Oscar Johnston, manager of the AAA cotton option school and a large Mississippi landowner, stated that "the sharecropper system is the fairest system that can be devised for labor engaged in the production of cotton."[62]

This was too much for Mitchell and East who sat down and penned a letter to Oscar Johnston on Clay East's Service Station stationary. They challenged Johnston to a bet. Not only were they willing to say that Thomas's observations were true for the Arkansas delta, but they bet "one of Mr. Roosevelt's 59 cent dollars" that the same conditions existed on Johnston's plantation. East and Mitchell rejected the idea that sharecroppers and tenant farmers' condition was the result of their own shiftlessness and argued that it was the "fault of a damnable system combining the worst features of feudalism with capitalistic exploitation."[63]

Johnston wrote back the next day asking East and Mitchell how they would run southern cotton farms. Specifically, how would they improve the cotton crop's market price? Johnston denied that his farm was like the one described by Thomas and invited East and Mitchell to drive down to have a look at his plantation. In the end, he said that he wanted to get rid of the sharecropping system but could not think of a way to replace it. Therefore, Johnston argued it was the best system for all parties.[64]

Johnston and the Tyronza socialists exchanged other letters, but only one still exists. On March 1, Mitchell wrote Johnston responding to a letter of February 24, in which Johnston stated that he had made an investigation of European farming and could find no cooperative farms like Mitchell had previously described. Mitchell, on March 1, wrote to say that Johnston's investigation was as incomplete as his "understanding of conditions in the South." The tone of this March 1 letter was not as cordial as the others had been, and Mitchell's sarcasm was biting. Mitchell argued that a man who thought southern sharecropping was the fairest system could obviously not be expected to find cooperative farming in Europe. This is the last extant letter between local Tyronza socialists and a planter before the union was founded.[65]

Planters turned their attention in two different directions. First, a group of planters met to hear Oscar Johnston speak, and according to newspaper accounts, these planters sent out an assurance to sharecroppers and tenant farmers that the planters would protect them. How many sharecroppers and tenant farmers were persuaded by this argument will never be known.[66]

Planters also turned their attention outward to convince the larger southern society that the real problem in the South was shiftless sharecroppers and the injustice that AAA contracts created for small farmers. Dr. Taft Butler made such an accusation in the February 20 issue of the *Arkansas Gazette*. Butler argued that the real southern injustice was the 1934 rental contract requiring thousands of small farmers, who had been planting only twenty-five to thirty percent of their cultivated land in cotton, to plow up the same share of their crop as the large planters who planted sixty to ninety-nine percent of their cultivated land in cotton.[67] The planter's shift of emphasis from sharecroppers and tenant farmers to small farmers was indicative of the underlying assumption in most planters' minds—sharecroppers and tenant farmers were shiftless. If they did not own farms, most planters believed it was their own fault.

Norman Thomas quickly became the center of controversy. Thomas's speech attracted numerous letters and criticisms in southern newspapers. On March 8, Thomas received a letter from George Morris, the assistant publisher for the *Memphis Commercial Appeal*. Morris argued, as had others, that there was no reason for a person to remain a tenant farmer unless he lacked "enterprise" to improve his condition. Morris suggested that any man could buy land cheap in the South and work his way up the agricultural ladder to become a landowner. Morris offered as an example the late R. E. Lee Wilson, who he claimed was the largest individual cotton farmer in the world. Morris argued that Wilson had reached his position of wealth and power even though he had begun as a tenant farmer. He finished his terse letter with a claim that the only reason that a man would be a tenant farmer would be because he lacked intelligence or ambition.[68] John C. Stevens, a merchant who claimed to have business contacts on the Mississippi delta plantation owned by Oscar Johnston, added that the real problem with sharecroppers was that they were the "most care-free people" with no responsibilities who had all their needs provided.[69] In a blatantly racist letter, George Parke, a freelance writer, argued that black tenant farmers had been better off in slavery, where planters had controlled their innate shiftlessness, immorality and cowardice.[70]

Thomas was shocked by these letters and argued that it was an insult to sharecroppers and tenant farmers to call them shiftless. He recounted the story of Ed Boston, a man he had met in Tyronza, who got up well before dawn every morning to travel to the river and work, a sixty-mile round trip, all because his landlord had taken his plot of land out of cultivation to meet AAA contract requirements. Thomas argued that tenant farmers and sharecroppers, instead of being shiftless, were hardworking men and women. Thomas also argued that what he had found in Arkansas was not exceptional. He cited other studies showing the southern tenancy system to be inhumane. He challenged planters to write laws giving their tenants legal protection instead of "pious good wishes." Thomas ended his rebuttal by returning to a point he made in his speeches: the problem was not the planters but the capitalist system, which had to be replaced.[71]

Excited finally to hear someone take their side in what they knew by experience to be an unjust situation, sharecroppers and tenant farmers began to write Norman Thomas, hoping he could help them find resources to get on their feet. Such letters would continue throughout the union's life. What is interesting in letters from sharecroppers and tenant farmers is their failure to mention socialism or radicalism. These sharecroppers and tenant farmers only wanted a fair chance to work hard and make a living for themselves within the tenant system. Ed Wilson, a sharecropper, wrote to Thomas in April to complain that he had no place to keep his possessions or wife and kids, and wanted to know if Thomas could help in getting him a tent to live in until he could find a place to work in the fall. Lois Bray also wanted help getting a new house and reporting a corrupt planter who was cheating his tenants. Thomas was not sure what to do with these pleas for help so he turned them over to Mitchell. Mitchell ignored them. His reasoning was not just callused. Although he may have hoped that such suffering would drive those suffering to socialism, in reality, if

Mitchell tried to help one family back to its feet he would be faced with an avalanche of requests without the financial resources he would have needed to assist those in need.[72]

There was one last set of reactions, from New Deal agencies. What he saw in the Arkansas delta horrified Norman Thomas, and turned all his moral venom on the one governmental agency he felt was responsible for the suffering. A few days after leaving Tyronza, Thomas wrote to Secretary of Agriculture Henry Wallace. Thomas laid out his case with great passion to Wallace. The system of sharecropping and tenant farming was a form of "peonage." The "abominable and indefensible system of landlordism" had to be ended. Thomas believed the AAA had made a bad situation even worse. Men, women, and children were so poor they could not afford clothes, and now because of the crop reduction schemes, planters were throwing their tenants "out on the road." He believed that landowners were reducing the number of sharecroppers and tenant farmers and increasing the amount of land farm workers had to tend, all so landowners could get a larger share of the government plow-up money. Former sharecroppers and tenant farmers were without hope. No industrial work was available for them, and more land was being taken out of production, which meant there would not be land for them to work. Thomas could not help commenting on the irony of reducing the cotton crop when so many children of tenant farmers and sharecroppers "run naked or clothed in rags or sugar sacking." Thomas did not blame Wallace for the inhuman situation he had found. Thomas knew that Wallace was a man deeply moved by the suffering of the poor everywhere; but he wanted Wallace to act. Thomas, always the consummate gentleman, would continue to attack Wallace and the AAA in mildly conciliatory terms for the next few weeks.[73]

Henry Wallace had spent a good portion of his life thinking about farming problems. As early as 1920 in his book *Agricultural Prices*, he had argued that the way to stabilize farm produce prices was to limit production. Wallace's ideas came to the attention of Rexford Guy Tugwell, an advisor to Franklin D. Roosevelt, who arranged a meeting between the two men. Roosevelt liked Wallace, and the following February he invited Wallace to become Secretary of Agriculture. Wallace crafted the Agricultural Adjustment Act, which he hoped would restore "reasonable parity" by providing farmers who agreed to produce less of certain basic commodities, including cotton, compensatory governmental payments. To protect tenants, the original plan called for all planters to give a portion of the parity check to their tenants equal to the percentage of the land under their care that was plowed up. Wallace trusted this plan would be fairest for all involved.[74]

Wallace revealed private and public personas in his response to Thomas's attacks. In private, Wallace was deeply concerned. He admitted there were sharecroppers and tenant farmers who had been thrown off the land because of the crop reduction program, and he truly wanted to prevent this. The issues of land ownership and rights were secondary to Wallace; he believed the issue at stake in the South was a human rights issue. At its heart, the issue was whether men and women would be given the right to live full and decent lives, which they controlled. Wallace was equally concerned that socialists and communists might weaken the government if this human rights issue was not dealt with immediately. Wallace wanted to see a committee set up that would coordinate relief for sharecroppers and tenant farmers. He felt strongly that someone from the Federal Emergency Relief Agency should be on the committee to represent such farmers, whom he felt would be forgotten by the departments of the Interior and Agriculture.[75]

In public, Wallace seemed to hold quite different positions. He defended the status quo. He ignored the human rights issues and interpreted the situation as simply a land problem. In public, Wallace argued that the poorer classes in the South had always existed, and while no one in America could ever be content until this situation was rectified, one could not blame Franklin Roosevelt's crop reduction plan. Wallace even argued that the crop reduction plan, which raised the price of cotton, had also decreased the number of evictions. Wallace hoped that in the near future a contract could be devised to protect all people involved in southern agriculture. The dye was cast. When faced with a socialist threat, Wallace reduced the issue of evictions to a question of land and property rights.[76]

It was never an absolute certainty that the Southern Tenant Farmers' Union would be founded. Although Thomas had wanted Mitchell and East to give up local politics and turn their attention to organizing sharecroppers and tenant farmers, they did not seem too interested in this approach to the serious situation in the Arkansas delta. Instead, Mitchell, in particular, believed that the revolution was right around the corner. East, on the other hand, seemed consumed with trying to provide for his family. One last event in the spring of 1934 would teach East and Mitchell that they had to do something to organize sharecroppers and tenant farmers.

The conciliatory terms that Thomas used when he attacked Wallace ended on March 10, 1934. Thomas had met Ed Boston and his family a month earlier on his Arkansas delta tour. Boston was known around the county as a hard-working person. In 1933, he had made $451.55 on which he had to feed a family of nine. This family's situation moved Thomas greatly, and all over the country Thomas told of Boston's plight.[77] On March 10, 1934, news reached Thomas that Ed Boston and his family had been evicted from the H. H. Howington farm near Tyronza. Arthur Ashlock, manager of the Howington farm, later said that he had evicted Boston for two reasons: Boston had refused to take part in the crop reduction plan of 1933; all through 1933, Boston refused to have his cotton ginned at the plantation gin, as required by his contract. Howington, who did not live on the farm, disputed Boston's character, saying that Boston was "one who had wasted his substance of livelihood instead of giving his wife and children the necessities to which I am sure they were entitled."[78]

Boston had been away in the woods gathering fuel at the time the eviction notice had been delivered. Mitchell, in a letter to Thomas, said this was probably providential or there might have been bloodshed. The day after Boston and his family were evicted, Mitchell went to their old cabin and found that another family had already moved in. Since three of Boston's children were ill with whooping cough, it was imperative to find them a safe, dry place to live. The first night they stayed with a sharecropper on another plantation who had also just received an eviction notice. Eventually Mitchell found the family a place south of Tyronza.[79]

On March 10, after receiving news of Boston's eviction, Thomas sent a telegraph to Henry Wallace. Thomas was almost frantic, feeling a tinge of personal responsibility. Had he not spoken to Boston and told his story all over the nation perhaps Boston and his family would not have been evicted. Thomas, almost screaming through the telegraph, pleaded with Wallace: "Can you not act at once?"[80]

Not content to wait on Wallace, Thomas wired Amberson in Memphis and asked him to get in touch with Roger Baldwin at the American Civil Liberties Union to see if he would personally defend Boston. Thomas also promised to raise money to defend Boston in the courts if necessary.[81] The story of Boston's eviction ran in numerous papers around the country, including the *New York Times*, which ran the story under the title, "Thomas Assails AAA in Wire to Wallace: Charges it has Added to Misery of Sharecroppers while Helping Landlords."[82] Thomas believed the Boston situation could become a test case for planters, and if someone did not stop them, they might use it to start a wave of evictions of sharecroppers. While Thomas overstated the extent of "conspiracy" in the evictions, he was not far off the mark. Evictions did increase.

With the national spotlight on his agency, Wallace could not afford to ignore the Boston situation. He quickly turned the investigation over to Cully Cobb who had been for many years the editor of the *Southern Ruralist*, a southern agricultural magazine. After he was appointed head of the cotton section of the Agricultural Adjustment Administration, Cobb intentionally identified with large planters who made up the vast majority of his readership. When he was placed in charge of the cotton section of the AAA he reportedly said that he wanted to do for planters what Alexander Hamilton had done for industrialists in the latter part of the eighteenth century. This pro-planter attitude would be obvious in his dealings with sharecroppers and tenant farmers.[83]

Cobb sent his assistant, E. A. Miller, to Tyronza to handle the Boston case. Miller came to investigate Boston's eviction and other claims of "wholesale evictions." After the first day of his two-day visit, Miller telegraphed a recommendation back to Wallace, suggesting that every planter who subscribed to the cotton reduction program be required immediately to file a list of his tenants from 1933 and 1934. Miller believed this would be important to "protect [the] program from unfavorable criticism and remove the temptation to displace tenants."[84] Miller also announced that he found no "wholesale chiseling" by Arkansas planters, who were, in fact, keeping the same number of tenants. Wallace jumped on this first day's report and announced that his man in the field had found no conspiracy of mass evictions as Norman Thomas had claimed. After one more day of touring the area, Miller returned to Washington, but not before having Boston sign a statement confirming that he had made a verbal agreement with Ashcock to leave the plantation at the end of 1934, at the time he was evicted.[85]

Mitchell was livid that Boston would sign such an agreement with a planter. For all practical purposes, the Boston case was dead; there would be no legal action. Mitchell now turned his attack on the investigation, calling it at best "superficial." In a letter to the *Arkansas Gazette*, Mitchell implied that Miller had simply listened to what the large planters had to say about evictions and reported it verbatim back to Washington. In the *American Guardian*, Mitchell claimed that the meeting between Miller and the landlords was "A Love Feast." Quoting from a survey of the Transient Bureau of Memphis records, Mitchell claimed that many of the 600 families on its rolls were from Tyronza. This seemed to Mitchell ample proof that Tyronza sharecroppers were being displaced. Mitchell also pointed out that those who remained on farms were actually receiving more land to farm, which was a violation of the AAA contract.[86] In the end, Mitchell believed that Miller's investigation had been predetermined. As Miller was leaving town, he stopped by Mitchell's shop and requested "that there not be any more complaint or disturbances" from the Tyronza area. Miller wanted to remind Mitchell that the landlords were his friends and that sharecroppers were a "shiftless lot." Mitchell reported that Miller even said, "there is no use of being concerned about them as they really don't count you know they are here to-day and gone to-morrow."[87] Did Miller really say these words to Mitchell? We will never know for sure, but they do demonstrate that Mitchell, as well as Thomas and Amberson, had come to believe that southern landowners exerted a powerful influence within the New Deal. Roosevelt needed southern votes in Congress, and he could not afford to offend them. Mitchell would never forget this lesson.[88]

Sharecropper home in eastern Arkansas. LIBRARY OF CONGRESS.

Sharecropper's shack near West Memphis, Arkansas. LIBRARY OF CONGRESS.

The families of evicted sharecroppers of the Dibble Plantation, Parkin, Arkansas. The Dibble Plantation, after pressure from the banks, charged that membership in the Southern Tenant Farmers Union was a conspiracy to retain their homes.
LIBRARY OF CONGRESS.

The families of evicted sharecroppers of the Dibble Plantation, Parkin, Arkansas.

LIBRARY OF CONGRESS.

The families of evicted sharecroppers of the Dibble Plantation, Parkin, Arkansas. LIBRARY OF CONGRESS.

Evicted Arkansas sharecropper, one of the more active of the union members, now building his new home at Hill House, Mississippi. LIBRARY OF CONGRESS.

Sharecroppers hold picket signs with, among others, "Help the Southern Tenant Farmers Union." LIBRARY OF CONGRESS.

H. L. Mitchell, Secretary of Southern Tenant Farmers Union. LIBRARY OF CONGRESS.

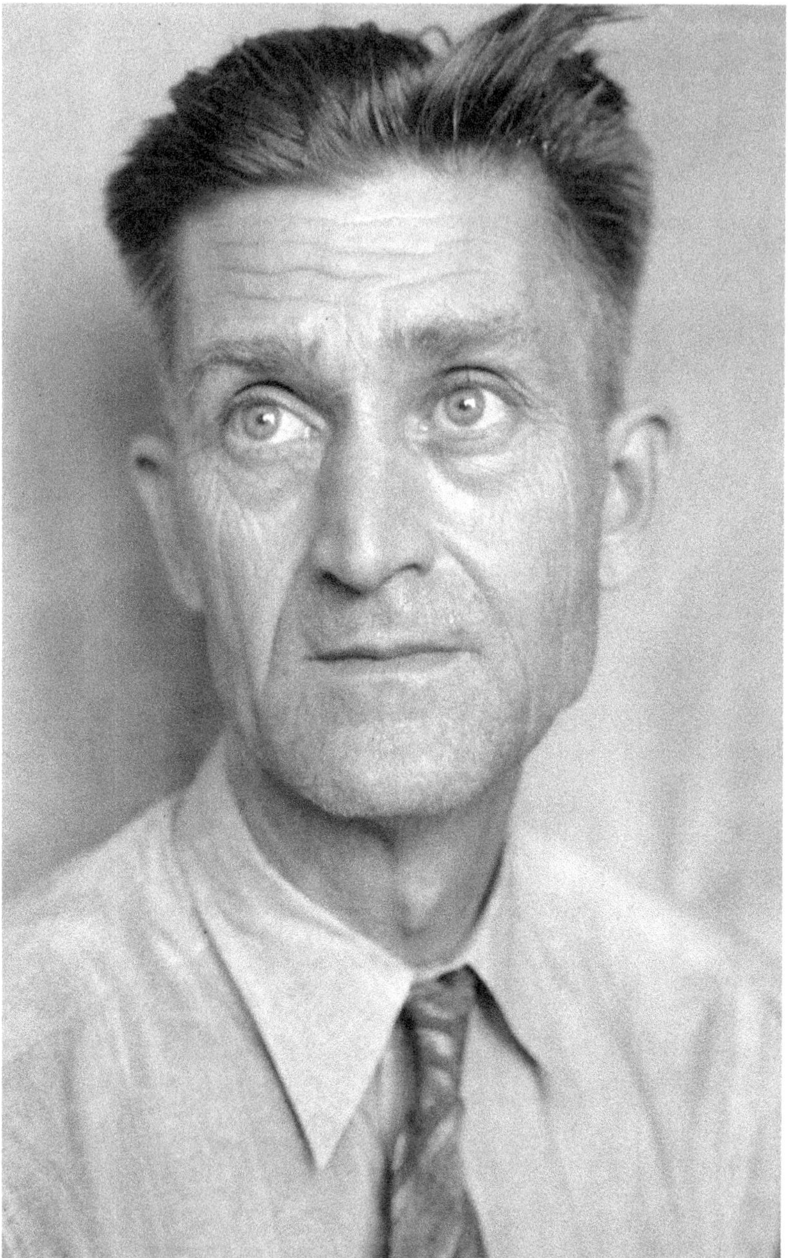

J. R. Butler, President of the Southern Tenant Farmer's Union.

LIBRARY OF CONGRESS.

CHAPTER THREE

THE BOSTON FAMILY HAD LOST ITS LAND, home, and livelihood, and there was nothing that Clay East or H. L. Mitchell could do. Their political contacts in the Roosevelt Administration had proven to be conservative protectors of the plantation system, and the sharecroppers and tenant farmers had failed to embrace their radical vision or to revolt. Mitchell and East had struggled for four months to bring revolution to Tyronza, but in the end, they failed. It was in the context of shattered hopes that these two young men turned their attention to the possibility of forming a union.

When Norman Thomas came to Tyronza in February 1934, after visiting sharecroppers and tenant farmers in the morning, he had stopped by East's house. Over a lunch prepared by Clay East's wife, the men discussed what Norman Thomas had seen; they also planned the rest of Thomas's visit to Arkansas. Towards the end of the meal, the men began to discuss what they could do to aid sharecroppers and tenant farmers. Thomas made it clear to them that it thrilled him that they were doing such great work in organizing the local Socialist Party, but he was not convinced that in the long run this would help the sharecroppers and tenant farmers. These poor men and women could not afford to vote; those who had their poll tax tickets usually had the tax paid by their landlords. Thomas believed that they needed a non-electoral solution. It was at this lunch that Thomas first suggested a sharecroppers' union.[1]

The idea intrigued Mitchell and East, but they did not know how to go about putting together a union. However, after the Boston affair, these two local socialists, under the direction of Norman Thomas, William Amberson, and other national and regional socialists, moved to form a union.

Their work would be difficult and had serious economic consequences. H. L. Mitchell and Clay East's business careers were destroyed by their Socialist Party work. The local Tyronza Baptist and Methodist women's organizations led a boycott of East's gas station and Mitchell's dry-cleaning business. In March, Mitchell reported that the "opposition" had bought out East's business. He was concerned that he might have to "unload" his own shop on them, but he hoped to be able to hold on.[2] By April 1934, Mitchell knew he was beat. The women running the boycott were very effective. They were quickly shutting off any means he had to make a living in the dry-cleaning business. He was troubled that those opposed to him had decided that it was cheaper and easier to "starve him out" rather than to buy his business.[3] He simply closed down his business in July.[4] Mitchell and East now found themselves without any income, and despair overcame them for the next few months.

East was restless after the loss of his business, and began to talk of leaving the area and quitting the movement. Mitchell was so concerned that he wrote a letter to Norman Thomas asking him to encourage East to go to the Rand School or stay in Tyronza and fight the good fight. Mitchell was frightened by the prospect of having to build the Socialist Party by himself. Thomas wrote East telling him he was one of the "bravest men" he had met in America. He commended East for being willing to give up everything for principles in the face of such pain and oppression. He asked East to stay in Tyronza and fight. Thomas, realizing that his words might be considered insensitive, stated later in the letter, "It's easy for me to sit here and advise you to keep up the fight at the front where it's hard . . ." In the end none of these words mattered. East was gone. His wife was not sure where he had gone but thought he might have gone to Arizona to see his brother and father who had moved there in 1927 looking for a new life. East traveled around the west for a while and returned to Tyronza for a short time. He bought a beauty parlor for his wife, hoping that she would be able to make enough money for her and their son to live on while he took a more active role in the movement. He worried about his family. He only wanted a good life for them, so he decided he had to get back into business. East bought a small gas station in Bartlett, Tennessee. From there he attempted to be involved in the movement. In 1936, East returned to

Arizona and was never active in the STFU again. While East was trying to find a new way to provide for his family, Mitchell carried on the work of forming the sharecroppers' union by himself.[5]

Thomas, Mitchell, and East had met in February and talked about forming a union, but by spring they had made little progress. East's leaving and his unpredictable behavior when he returned distracted Mitchell from the work of forming a union. But East was not totally to blame for the failure to form a union. Mitchell was young and easily distracted. He put much of his energy after the February meeting with Thomas into two issues. The first was a land offer near Hot Springs, Arkansas where the Arkansas Socialist party wanted to establish a labor school. G. M. Yates, a rich landowner, offered the socialists four hundred acres. Mitchell was incredibly excited and immediately began to plan the labor school.

Before Mitchell could ask the Socialist Party's national office to commit money to the labor school, he had to find someone to look over the land. Mitchell called on his friend, Ward H. Rodgers, who was a Methodist minister and radical socialist. Rodgers was born in Texas and lived in Oklahoma as a young man. He spent a couple of years at the Central State Teachers College in Alva, Oklahoma where he received a B. A. When he did not find a teaching job, he decided to enter the Methodist ministry. He attended a year at Iliff School of Theology at Denver University, but the second year he moved to Vanderbilt University where he studied under the Social Gospel theologian Alva Taylor.

In 1933 the Methodist church appointed Rodgers to a church in Winona, a small town in southern Missouri. The area bishop soon sent him to Arkansas where he worked a circuit around Mount Magazine in northwestern Arkansas. He had three churches: one on top of the mountain, the other on the south side and one in the little town of Pumpkin Center. He would walk for miles from church to church because he could not afford to put gas in his Whippet. He later resigned from the churches because he felt he could not rightfully take money from his poverty-stricken parishioners.

Rodgers had converted to socialism while in Denver, and had met Norman Thomas at Vanderbilt in 1932. He had met Mitchell at the Arkansas Socialist convention in 1934 in Tyronza. It was at this meeting that he became interested in the sharecroppers and tenant farmers. As a dedicated member of the radical wing of the party, Rodgers was looking for the group in American society that would be the spark for socialist revolution. In Mitchell he found a kindred spirit. After looking over the land, he reported that the offer was for four hundred acres of which about two hundred were suitable for cultivation. He also found plenty of timber to use for building structures on the campus. There were herds of goats, cattle, and tools, which Yates planned to turn over to Mitchell.

Mitchell wrote to Thomas wanting direction again. He wanted to know if Thomas would help obtain financial support and publicity for the new school. He also wanted to know if the farm should be under the control of the Socialist Party or an independent group, which the Socialist Party could then control.[6] Thomas quickly wrote back and stated that the school would need to be a separate independent corporation but controlled by the Socialist party. He suggested that the Party could control the labor school by a provision in the charter that the majority or even two-thirds of the school directors should be members of the Socialist Party. Thomas found the news of the labor school exciting, and Mitchell's enthusiasm encouraged him. But Thomas cautioned that the school might compete with Commonwealth College in Mena, Arkansas, and warned against allowing this to happen. Instead, Thomas suggested that the school should model itself after the Danish Folk School, where farmers came for picnics and short sessions on farming and labor issues. Thomas even offered to raise money for the school if the leaders would send him a budget. The promise of the school encouraged other socialists such as Clarence Senior, William Amberson, and Clark Waldron, all of whom wanted to be actively involved in making it a success.

When Mitchell sent a budget for $1500, Thomas began to worry. He asked Clark Waldron, a Missouri socialist, to go to Arkansas and "watch that school proposition carefully." Thomas was concerned about the small budget that Mitchell had proposed. He doubted if Mitchell truly understood what he was doing. Thomas wanted to know if that amount of money was enough to start and run a school, and he wanted to know if the school was the best way to use the money in Arkansas.[7]

While Mitchell and Rodgers worked to secure the land for the labor school, the Tyronza Socialist local and the Memphis local of the League for Industrial Democracy were conducting a survey of conditions in the Arkansas and Mississippi delta region. The survey was the idea of William Amberson and had originally surfaced in February.[8] Amberson then wrote to Clarence Senior, the National Secretary for the Socialist party, to report on activities in Memphis. Amberson stated that he was going to Tyronza the next day to convince the local to take part in the survey in order "to determine the human and social results of the crop reduction program." Particularly he wanted to know if the AAA had led to landowners decreasing the number of sharecroppers and tenant farmers, and increasing the work for those remaining. Amberson was insecure with this survey idea and wanted to know whether Senior thought that this was "good socialist strategy." We do not have Senior's response, but the survey began.[9] They agreed to use out-of-work Socialist Party members who were "sufficiently intelligent to write down the necessary information."[10]

In March 1934, Amberson was able to write Thomas with some very preliminary findings from a small survey of those sharecroppers and tenant farmers present at the survey planning meeting. They found that black tenants were replacing "considerable numbers" of white families. It was possible for landowners to pay their black tenants less, and therefore make a larger profit. They later visited one plantation where eighteen white families had been evicted and replaced by black families. They found that the Poinsett County sheriff was concerned about the evictions, but when it came time to evict the tenants, he had few choices and continued evictions. As they had suspected, landlords were violating AAA contracts. Landlords were increasing the acreage farmed per family which was a violation of the AAA contract. The situation seemed to be reaching a critical stage. Mrs. Alex East, the relief administrator in the county, had two thousand families for whom she had received an allotment of six thousand dollars for two weeks. This meant that one-third of the county was on direct relief. This, Amberson argued, was because of the increased number of sharecroppers and tenant farmers being thrown off the land. Finally, they found that the greatest abuses of the crop reduction contracts were occurring on large plantations. Most of the smaller plantations were trying to fulfill their AAA contracts. The survey teams continued to gather data.[11]

With these preliminary findings as their guide, Amberson and the Tyronza Socialist Party local set out to find more evidence. Amberson and the Tyronza socialists were able to get a small group of men to work in Memphis on the survey. Amberson trained them to interview displaced farmers in Memphis and then send them back to their communities to collect information. Soon, though, the men in Tyronza who were helping gather data became distressed and weary and were on the verge of giving up. They were unable to see the point of wasting their time on a survey when their families were starving and barely clothed. In late March, Amberson told Mitchell to pay the workers a small sum for each information card they were able to collect.[12]

On April 8, 1934, Amberson sent Buck Jones, an out-of-work tenant, to survey Oscar Johnson's plantation in Mississippi. What unfolded was a bizarre story that gives a small glimpse of the tension surrounding the STFU's birth. In late March or early April, Amberson and others journeyed to Oscar Johnson's plantation and declared the visit a "great success." From interviews of over one hundred families, they found that the landlords were not reducing crops for tenant families in compliance with AAA contracts. They found that the acreage was reduced about sixteen percent instead of the forty percent required by law. This meant that tenant families were doing more work than they were supposed to be doing and receiving less money. This was important evidence, and they wanted to guard this information closely for fear that Johnson might have a chance to fix the problems before the news became public.[13]

On a second visit, the local sheriff arrested Buck Jones. When Amberson and others went to see Johnson, the local sheriff treated them roughly. Amberson called Johnson and asked to see him about Jones; Johnson told Amberson and his crew to meet him at a designated location. When Amberson and the others arrived, officials told them that Johnson was sick and that they would need to see the town's sheriff instead. An hour later the sheriff showed up at the meeting place. After introducing everyone and shaking hands, the sheriff pulled out his pistol; other deputies came out of hiding with their pistols drawn. The law enforcement agents searched Amberson and his group. After not finding any weapons, the sheriff seemed confused, and Amberson was finally able to convince the sheriff that Johnson had invited them. The sheriff bought them coffee, apologized, and explained that informants had identified them as John Dillinger and his gang. The group was finally able to get Jones out of jail and leave town before any other problems arose.[14]

When the report was finished, it included data on five hundred families in Arkansas, Missouri, Tennessee, and Mississippi, as well as transient families in Memphis. Thomas was thrilled about the work and sent fifty dollars to support it. He also decided to publish the findings as a League for Industrial Democracy pamphlet that he believed would help "keep up the fight with the Department of Agriculture."[15]

When the report was finally printed, the Tyronza socialists and the Memphis League for Industrial Democracy concluded that the acreage reduction program had indeed reduced the number of families working on cotton farms. Section 7(a) of the AAA contract told the producer to endeavor to keep the same number of tenants on his farm as before and to allow them to stay rent free. They found that many sharecroppers and tenant farmers were being kicked off the land. For the year 1933, the survey revealed that thirty-seven percent of families had plowed up no land. Fifty percent had plowed up all of their land. Twenty-six percent had plowed up some land, but less than the twenty-five percent specified by contract. Twenty-seven percent plowed up more than twenty-five percent. Ten percent plowed up the twenty-five percent required by contract. In the end, the survey revealed that between fifteen and twenty percent were kicked off the land. The authors observed that there was a shift from white labor to black labor who could be paid less. The Lee Wilson and Company Plantation in Mississippi County, Arkansas, advertised for laborers, but specifically stated that no white families need apply. There was also a shift from tenancy to day labor with fewer obligations on the landlord. Typical was the R. T. Kuhn Plantation in Crittenden County, Arkansas. According to a report, this plantation had "largely or completely eliminated" sharecropping and moved to day labor. One of the Tyronza investigators posing as a farmer seeking a sharecrop approached one of the Kuhn riding bosses, who told the investigator: "We don't intend to give these niggers a share-crop. We're going to wait until it is too late to get a crop anywhere else, and then work them as day labor at 6 bits a day."[16]

Local socialists discovered other issues that suggested a pattern of oppression. It was common practice for plantation stores to charge ten cents on the dollar interest on all furnishings. When investigators compared actual prices in commissary stores to those of cash stores, they found that commissary stores regularly overcharged their customers for the same goods. For example, in one commissary store a twenty-four-pound bag of flour was $1.05 but only $.95 in the cash store.

The survey also revealed that neither black nor white families had attained the educational status of urban workers. Of the sharecroppers' children who were surveyed, 475 out of 675 were out of school. Sharecroppers and tenant farmers gave many reasons for their children not being in school: lack of schoolbooks, clothing, and shoes, failure of bus services, and closed schools. The authors concluded that the children of sharecroppers would never have the opportunity to advance beyond the life of their parents if they did not have access to free public education.[17]

The survey was a great success, and it reaffirmed for Thomas and other socialists the urgency of forming a union. By early May, Thomas was troubled about "the Arkansas situation." Thomas's major concern continued to be the budget proposed by Mitchell, who had asked for $1500 to begin his school. Thomas wrote to William Amberson and Missouri socialist Clark Waldron to obtain their candid opinion as to whether this would be an adequate amount to secure the land, build the school, and staff it with qualified people. At the heart of his concern was the question whether the school project would hamper fundraising for a sharecropper union if they could ever get Mitchell to focus on that project.[18]

In early June, Thomas had received a letter from Clay East, who had expressed some doubt about the proposed school. He was concerned about the lack of a plan, effective leadership, and money. Thomas was now concerned with the information that Mitchell was giving him. When Martha Johnson wrote to Thomas that she opposed the school, that seemed to kill Thomas's enthusiasm for the idea.[19] But by July Thomas's concerns no longer mattered; Yates had backed out of the deal, killing the school, much to the relief of Thomas and other Socialist Party leaders.[20]

Norman Thomas increasingly worried about sticking his neck out for Mitchell and East. He had suggested in his first meeting with them that what was needed was a union in which sharecroppers and tenant farmers could shape their own future through collective action. But these two young socialists had been easily distracted. In late June, Thomas wrote Mitchell and said he wanted to send money but did not know exactly what was going on in the state and was concerned that the men might not use the money properly.[21] In a letter the Johnsons wrote for Thomas, they told Mitchell that Thomas was concerned about starting a national campaign to raise money and then have the "whole business fall apart."[22] Thomas did not think that Mitchell was the best man for the job, but then he had no one who knew the local situation as well as Mitchell. In the end, Mitchell would become head of the union, although as late as 1939 Thomas was hoping to get rid of Mitchell in favor of a better man who could be more easily controlled.[23]

The main issue that worried Thomas and other socialist leaders was the money shortage. Thomas wanted to do something to alleviate the sharecroppers and tenant farmers' suffering and wanted to help them raise money. On March 26, 1934, he had made his first offer to help raise money. In later years, he would regret this offer, as the STFU never became self-sufficient. Throughout the rest of the spring and early summer, Clarence Senior, Clark Waldron, and Norman Thomas raised money for the school plan, survey, and to form the union. But their concern over Mitchell and East's ability to work efficiently made them doubt whether they were using their time wisely.[24]

Thomas's ambivalence about Mitchell and East's leadership demonstrates the problem the Socialist Party had in controlling the STFU. Historians have argued over this question for almost forty years. The issue revolves around the meaning of the term "control." If "control" means the Socialist Party established all STFU policies from beginning to end, then of course, the Socialist Party never controlled the STFU. However, the Socialist Party was very influential in the union. Socialist leaders such as Thomas, Senior, and Waldron raised most of the money for the union in its early months.[25] The Johnsons encouraged Mitchell to stay in Arkansas and to work on the union when he was depressed and wanted to leave the state.[26] Thomas and Amberson so influenced Mitchell that he was always adapting himself to whatever he felt would make them happy. When the work was just beginning, Mitchell adapted his radical socialism to the more moderate socialism of Thomas and Amberson. In a letter written in July 1934, Mitchell revealed clearly the massive influence the Socialist Party, particularly its Progressive wing, had on him and others in Arkansas who were working on the Union. Mitchell wrote to Thomas with a proposed budget for one-hundred-fifty dollars that Thomas had promised to raise for him. Mitchell told him that J. R. Butler and J. O. Green, two local socialists, were ready to go to work for the Union immediately. After listing some preliminary contacts they had made, Mitchell declared, "I am sure we can fix things so that it won't look as tho' these things are direct party activities."[27] They seemed unable to conceptualize the union outside of Socialist Party control. The union was, in these early days, the Party; and the Party was the union. Even after the union was founded and Mitchell wanted it to be a secret order, he changed his approach when told to do so by Thomas.[28] Thus, the Socialist Party, and particularly certain Progressive leaders, were instrumental in the union's founding; without the Party the union might have faltered at the very beginning.

Other projects distracted the Tyronza socialists, and for many months the lone voice pushing for the sharecroppers and tenant farmers' union was Norman Thomas. In Arkansas, no one was sure what a sharecroppers' union would look like or how to establish one.[29] Mitchell seemed to have originally thought that the union would be a new way to get members into the Tyronza Socialist Party local. In April 1934, he suggested to Thomas that they should wait on founding the union until the fall when the union could "dictate" the terms of the next contract and gain more sharecroppers by taking such a strong stance.[30] At the same time, J. Clark Waldron, a Missouri socialist who was trying to raise money for the sharecroppers' union, thought that it could be used as a platform for taking legal actions against the evictions of sharecroppers and tenant farmers. By July 1934, Thomas became fed up with all of the indecision and wanted some immediate demands drawn up. Clay East finally admitted in June that no one in Tyronza really knew what to do to make the union legal or how to draw up concrete plans, and he requested help.[31]

When Mitchell finally drew up a document entitled "Outline of Proposed Union," he sent it to Amberson and Thomas, anticipating quick support.[32] In the document, Mitchell laid out the union's aims and plans. He was still firmly committed to a militant philosophy as he wrote this document, believing that class conflict was inevitable and that it would end in class war. Mitchell began the document by recognizing that there was an "increase in conflict" between "those who work for a living" and those "who live on the labor of others." This was a struggle that he believed had to continue until workers and farmers united as a class and took over "the means of creating the wealth of the world." He then drew on his fundamentalist heritage and appealed to the Biblical golden rule. If all would "do unto the other as they wanted done to them," Mitchell was sure that this would lead to an acceptance of the cooperative way of life and "the abolition of the system of greed and profit." He then laid out an ultimatum. If the union came under attack it would not hesitate to use "whatever means are available for our protection." Membership would be open only to men eighteen years and older. All races or creeds could join. The only restrictions were aimed at women and those who "made their living off the labor of others."[33]

When William Amberson read this he was not happy. He wrote Senior and Thomas requesting that they write a constitution for the union. Amberson was frustrated that the proposal did not contain a program of immediate demands and only seemed to stress future revolution. Amberson even reported that he told Mitchell that there was "no use asking capitalism to incorporate the revolution." Amberson wanted the union to have specific and immediate demands and to function like a labor union, not a conduit for the Socialist Party. In his letter to Thomas, Amberson confessed that he did not think that Mitchell had the "background and education" to plan the union in a practical way. He even wanted to bring in a more experienced person to organize the Union. In a moment of rare despair, which in many ways proved to be prophetic, Amberson admitted that a union probably could not hold the sharecroppers and tenant farmers together, even if it were headed by the most experienced person. But he quickly shook off the despair and announced his allegiance to the union idea as long as Thomas stayed on the job.[34]

Thomas soon wrote Mitchell to tell him that the union would need to have some immediate demands built into its constitution and program. As late as August, 1934, Mitchell was still fighting the call for practical demands. Amberson, building on the long heritage of agrarian cooperative reform, was trying to get Mitchell to set up cooperative stores in which sharecroppers and tenant farmers could buy their goods at a lower price without having to pay exorbitant interest to merchants. Mitchell did not think that this would be a good idea because "the time is short." By this, he meant that the revolution would come soon, and cooperative stores would be a waste of time. Mitchell's commitment to radical Marxist theory over the pragmatic daily operations of the union flabbergasted Amberson. In a September news release about the union, Mitchell stated that the "demands of the union will be worked out from time to time by the membership as the occasion warrants."[35]

It would be late 1934 or 1935 before the leaders of the union would draft immediate demands and a constitution. In the meantime, tenant farmers and sharecroppers were not willing to wait on Mitchell or the Socialist Party. They were living in the daily hell of tenancy and wanted to do something, anything, to protect their children.

The sharecroppers and tenant farmers' story begins on the Fairview Plantation owned by Hiram Norcross. Norcross had been a lawyer for the Portland Cement Company in Kansas City, Missouri before moving to Arkansas and buying some forty-five-hundred acres of land from John Emrich, who owned the Tyronza bank and the large plantation commissary store in downtown Tyronza.[36]

Alex East, after losing his farm, went to work as plantation manager for Norcross. East furnished credit to sharecroppers and tenant farmers based on one dollar per acre. Being a compassionate man, East always wanted to make sure that Norcross's tenants had enough to live on until the end of the season. When Norcross found out that East had provided furnishings for almost sixteen hundred acres more than he owned, Norcross was outraged. He sent out a team to survey each man's land. Norcross then arbitrarily told some of the sharecroppers and tenant farmers to leave. He also told them that they were only going to get one third of the government plowup money, although the AAA contract stated that they were entitled to half.

There were about one hundred families on the Fairview Plantation, and many of them were growing weary of Norcross. In the spring and summer of 1934, some of the men began to meet behind the big barn on the plantation to discuss how they could obtain enough money to protect their families and acquire their rightful share of the plowup money. In these early meetings, Burt Williamson, a 250-pound sharecropper with a strong opinion on current events, suggested reviving the Ku Klux Klan. This time, he argued, the Klan would consist of both black and white men and would be used to take care of any planters who would not treat their sharecroppers fairly. Williams suggested that stringing Norcross to a tree would make him an example to other planters to treat sharecroppers and tenant farmers with fairness and respect. This appeal to violence was a very southern appeal and must have resonated in his listener's ears.[37]

Alvin Nunnaly, one of the early members of the Arkansas Socialist Party who lived on John Emrich's plantation, which adjoined Norcross's, also began to meet with the Fairview group. Nunnaly had remembered the Farmers' Union, which had a large following in Lawrence County, Arkansas. From his experience in the Farmers' Union, Nunnaly wanted to form a legal organization to deal with the troubles that the Fairview tenants were having. Nunnaly advocated calling on the Farmers Educational and Cooperative Union of America to help them organize. He even got Mitchell to help him send a letter to John Simpson to form a local of the Farmers' Union. A Farmers' Union representative came down from Jonesboro, Arkansas, and had a meeting, but little came of it. Most of the men who joined the Union were planters, and they left sharecroppers and tenant farmers out. Over time, Nunnaly became something of the leader of this rag tag group of men sneaking around the barn to secret meetings. Thus, when Mitchell and Thomas started talking about a union, they did not have to persuade the Fairview Plantation tenants of its value. These men had been looking for an organization to help them for months.[38]

On July 13, 1934, the sharecroppers and tenant farmers finally met with the Tyronza socialists at the Sunnyside school on the edge of the Fairview Plantation. Usually used for a "holy roller" church house, the school, filled with ten white men and seven black men, was lit with the dim light of two borrowed oil burning lamps. It would be easy to say that the STFU arose out of a rank and file revolt. Mitchell asserts this in many later accounts. Downplaying the active role he had in the union, he credits the sharecroppers and tenant farmers with calling the first meeting. In this later version, he and East are simply caught up in the flow of history initiated by others. But in a 1936 memo written for Howard Kester's eyes only, Mitchell told a different story. The sharecroppers and tenant farmers had been meeting secretly for a few months, but the July 13 meeting to initiate the first local was, according to Mitchell, a well-planned secret meeting. Mitchell reported that on that hot sultry night he sent word to a "picked group of men" to meet at nine o'clock at the schoolhouse. Clay East and Ward Rodgers confirmed this when each remembered meeting in June, 1934, to form the union in Mitchell's old Moon car. East said in typically blunt fashion that it was a "bunch of bull" that the croppers called the meeting.[39] They were driving to Charlie McCoy's place in Trumann, Arkansas, when Mitchell told Clay East that he was going to be the Union's president and appointed himself secretary. Rodgers, Butler, Amberson, and Nunnaly were all appointed to be on the Executive Board.[40] Instead of being spectators caught in the flow of history, Mitchell was the active agent in forming the STFU. Why would he construct such an alternative narrative? One possibility is the changed context in which he was telling his story. While speaking on college campuses in the 1960s Mitchell witnessed massive social change and being the good socialist and ardent salesman, it is possible that he would have constructed his narrative framing the earlier revolt as a spontaneous rising by the masses in order to help the new revolution find inspiration in the old one.

What then is authentic about this first meeting? We know the first meeting occurred. On July 25, 1934, Mitchell wrote to Amberson to report that they had formed the first group "down on the Fairview Plantation.[41] Mitchell always reported that he and East arrived late, but East denies this. Whenever they arrived, they later agreed that the speeches were given as recorded. Burt Williamson is usually reported to have been the first to speak; he told the group about his plan to revive the Klan. In later versions of the STFU's origins, Mitchell would omit this part. Again, the 1960s Civil Rights context may give a clue as to why he would leave out a white man calling for a revival of the Klan to begin systematic lynching. Nunnaly next addressed the group and argued for a legal and lawful organization. Nunnaly said he did not believe that secret organizations were the American way to settle differences. He was also afraid that the Klan might scare blacks away, and he was convinced that the issues that hobbled sharecroppers and tenant farmers could only be settled if black and white sharecroppers worked together.

After these two men spoke, the sharecroppers and tenant farmers voted to form a legal union. Next the men needed to justify an integrated union. Mitchell and the others had predetermined this. Two men spoke for a racially integrated union, led by Burt Williams. He told the white men present that it was time to forget the past. He argued that they were all in the same boat and there should be just one union. He asked every white man if he agreed, and every man said yes or nodded his head. Then a dignified aging black man stood up to address the crowd. Isaac Shaw was in his mid- to late-fifties and had seen a lot in his life. When his deep, rich, and melodious voice broke the silence of the night in that shadowy schoolroom he said: "Gentlemen, you have made the right decision. You have agreed that this organization should be legal; you have agreed that it should be for all the sharecroppers whether they are black or white." He then told them of the Elaine Massacre in Phillips County, Arkansas, when black sharecroppers tried to form a union without white help. He said he would fight for the Union and that black men needed white men as much as white men needed black men. Silence followed as he took his seat. Nunnaly then called on East and Mitchell to speak. East told them that the leaders would incorporate the union under state law, and that they were the first local of a union that would grow to include the whole South.[42]

These men who were present at the first meeting would not have believed that the union would live only a few years, and that all their dreams would be destroyed by the mechanization of farming and the enclosure of southern farms, which made sharecroppers and tenant farmers obsolete. But they did not know this that hot July night; they only knew that they were going to take care of their families. Everything else was inconsequential.

East and Mitchell believed that this was the beginning of revolution in the South. They believed that soon every state would have a branch of the union and the evil capitalist system of farming, which exploited poor farmers and made them ignorant, would be replaced by a cooperative commonwealth in which men and women lived together on cooperative farms without the profit motive and greed. But that was the future. They had formed the union that Norman Thomas assured would help sharecroppers. They were fighting for the revolution that would bring forth a new day.

The union's origins were not in a simple indigenous uprising as so many historians and participants have claimed. While there were distinct local actors in the founding of the union, there were also many other groups. The Socialist Party wanted to build its southern base, and later, it wanted to help sharecroppers and tenant farmers with cooperative farming. Mitchell and East, two idealistic young men, wanted to see the end of what they felt was a vicious economic system. There were also the sharecroppers and the tenant farmers. This group was not monolithic. On one side stood those who were willing to use violence to settle the payment problems that arose on the Fairview Plantation. Alvin Nunnaly persuaded another group to form a legal organization, which they believed would end the injustices of AAA policies. Each of these groups had its own vision of what the STFU should be. What unified them was their commitment to fighting against Norcross and the AAA.

The Progressive wing of the Socialist Party represented by men like Norman Thomas, William Amberson, Clark Waldron, and Clarence Senior, was also central to the founding of the union. They wanted to shape the Union and use it for their own purposes. While H. L. Mitchell wanted historians to remember him as one of these Progressives, the truth is he started as a radical Militant socialist—far closer to the communists than the socialists. Mitchell in time became the ever-dutiful pragmatist, proving willing to change his ideological views to get the work of the union done. His single-minded concern for the men and women of the Arkansas delta would strengthen in the months after the union's founding as violence began against him and the men and women he was trying to save. The union would always have inner tensions because these diverse forces present in the forming of the union were in constant conflict. The story of the STFU is not the story of constant victory over the powers of evil; instead, it is the human story of men and women struggling from their own perspective to care for their families and friends and to empower themselves. In the end, they were defeated.

But before this defeat, the tenant farmers joined the movement in droves. What was it that led illiterate and semiliterate god-fearing sharecroppers and tenant farmers to join a Union led by radical socialists? What led whites and blacks to sit on the same benches together in churches and schoolhouses in town after town? Why did they join the STFU?

CHAPTER FOUR

GRANVILLE WHITTIKER SAT PENSIVELY in a torn and tattered chair in front of a window in his dilapidated house looking out over the old Main Street of Edmondson, Arkansas. Main Street, which at one time had been bustling with businesses and people, was now empty. The road was squeezed in between tiny rundown houses and expansive soybean fields. As he sat in his home on that hot and blustery summer day in 1992, Whittiker was proud that he had never been farther than ten miles from his home. At eighty-six, he was happy to have his forty acres and to have his family around him. But times were still hard and he was barely able to make ends meet by renting his land to a man who planted soy beans on it.

Whittiker had lived long enough to see many wondrous and many tragic events in the life of this little town. Although he could not remember the exact day in 1911 when the town of Edmondson was incorporated, his father had told him many times of that day's excitement when a few hundred black men and women who had been buying up the land since the 1880s finally had enough land and people to become a town. Because it was so susceptible to flooding these former slaves and their children were able to buy this land cheap. In the early days of the twentieth century their gamble paid off when the federal and state governments set up the levee systems that kept the White and Mississippi Rivers from overrunning their banks. Granville remembered back seventy years when all the men and women in this completely black delta town owned and operated the businesses on Main Street, as well as the fertile land around it. Cotton was in the last days of what had once been a very profitable kingdom, and these men and women were on top of the world.

Granville remembered when that world began to come apart. He recalled the mid-1920s, when a white man from Proctor, Arkansas, made a deal with Anthony Flemming of the Edmondson Home Improvement Corporation. The black men and women who owned their land were not welcome in the county seat of Marion, where they had to pay their annual property and poll taxes, so the white man offered to take their money to the tax collector for them. Granville remembered the late 1920s and early 1930s when the landowners realized that the white man had not used their money to pay taxes, but instead had bought their land, which the state had declared delinquent for failure to pay taxes. Granville Whittiker also remembered the day C. A. Whithers and Issac Shaw told the new tenant farmers about the coming of the Kingdom of the Lord and His new instrument of mercy, the Southern Tenant Farmers' Union, complete with appropriate Bible text: "And you shall take possession of the land and live in it, for I have given the land to you to possess it."[1] This promise became Granville Whittiker's hope. Whittiker wanted to hold onto his land. He joined the STFU with great hope, believing that the Union would help him and his friends control the changes sweeping through their town. Eventually Granville Whittiker became disillusioned with Withers and "that crowd." "They meant well," but the white man from Proctor was willing to shoot Union men, and the Union never had a chance. It was the late 1960s before Granville Whittiker was able to buy back his forty acres. Today he rents it to the white man's son, who continues to live in the legacy of racism and hatred that his father left him. Granville Whittiker's experience was the exception. He found a way to regain the land. But the majority of black and white men and women who were trapped in the sharecropping system were not so lucky. Like Whittiker, many of them shared a longing, a dream, to go onto the land and take possession. They also wanted a way to support their families and to give their children a better life than they had. These dreams, for most, were not only deferred, they were destroyed.[2]

We know little of how union members responded to social change that was occurring all around them. Why did thousands of men and women join the STFU? What were the factors that led them to this union? More importantly, what did the union mean to these men and women? These men and women brought with them a specific religious culture to the union. Members made sense out of massive social changes going on around them, according to a particular religious worldview. They also used this worldview as the basis for their attempt to change their world.

Within the first year and a half of the union's existence, its headquarters was receiving hundreds of letters a month from sharecroppers and tenant farmers. Many of these men and women wrote their letters on paper bags and old cotton receipts. In these letters, union members shared stories of hope and despair. They told of their deepest longings and the most mundane daily events of their lives. They also shared the multiplicity of reasons they joined the union.

People joined the STFU to redress specific grievances and obtain immediate assistance. But they also brought to the union a deeply felt set of religious assumptions that shaped all they did. Most obviously, men and women joined the STFU in hopes of meeting their family's immediate needs. Acquiring food and clothes was a constant struggle. Writers of the period were shocked at the nature of the food eaten by sharecroppers and tenant farmers, whose basic diet consisted of salt meat, corn or flour bread, and sorghum. Very few locally grown vegetables were available because cotton production consumed most of the land. The average sharecropper and tenant lived on an advance of thirteen dollars per month, and this money had to be used for food, clothes, medicine, and all other family needs. In a 1933 survey of purchases made by sharecroppers and tenant farmers in Arkansas commissaries, T. J. Woofter, Jr., coordinator of Rural Research for the Works Project Administration (WPA), found that monthly sharecroppers and tenant farmers spent 64.4 percent of their money on food and 14.2 percent on clothing. This left 21.4 percent of their monthly advance for other needs.[3] In real dollars the sharecroppers and tenant farmers spent $8.37 a month on food and $1.86 a month on clothing, leaving only $2.77 dollars for other needs and emergencies.

Letters in the STFU files are painful reminders of what these figures meant to sharecroppers and tenant farmers. Issac Shaw, one of the union's founders, told of an Earle, Arkansas, family forced to collect animals from the highway after it had been accidentally killed. He reported that the family had found a pig dead in the road and had taken it home to eat in order to survive. He also reported that the husband of this family had later come across a snake with a dead turtle in its mouth. After chasing the snake away, he carried the turtle home for his wife to prepare.[4]

J. L. Lynn, one of the early members of the union's second local in Truman, Arkansas, wrote to H. L. Mitchell asking for five dollars to buy corn. He said his family had not had any corn in months. Lynn claimed they were without a penny to their name. He concluded by saying he was in the worst shape he had ever been in his life, but he hoped that Mitchell would not think "hard" of him. As he said, "I have done the best I can."[5]

In the midst of moving from one landlord to another, Will Washington wrote to Mitchell asking if the union could "let me have some groceries. Am without food an no monie to by. . . ."[6] John Robinson, in a fit of desperation, asked Mitchell to "do what you can at once." The weather was bad and he needed money for his wife and kids to eat for a few days.[7] Clara Jones wrote Mitchell explaining that her members were in such trouble that they could no longer help each other. They were angry and desperate. They had written for help three times previously to no avail. She wanted Mitchell to "please attend to this at once."[8] Letters from these men and women were full of desperation.

Although many men and women wrote on behalf of themselves and their families, the vast majority of letters concerning food were from people writing for friends. Ammie Love, an Earle, Arkansas, secretary, wanted to know if the union could help Longo Burns who had broken his leg and could not buy food. Nathan Wiley of Widner, Arkansas, wanted to know if anything could be done to get food to Arch Xollie, his wife, and their six children who had "already had to sell what he had around him to get something to eat."[9]

Not only did sharecroppers and tenant farmers need help getting food, they also needed help finding clothing. Charlie and Rosie Clayton hoped the union would help them get clothes for their seven children when they wrote to the STFU in 1935. They reported that they had four girls and three boys between the ages of six weeks and fourteen years. Each needed clothes and shoes to help them get through the upcoming winter months.[10] Mary Lee Moore of Turell, Arkansas, wrote, "I am already suffering for food and clothes." She reported that her landlord would throw anyone off his place who complained about conditions.[11] One anonymous sharecropper wrote from Altheimer, Arkansas, in 1937 to say that he wanted a "better living." He reported to the union, "I am naked, at this rate I owe a big debt, now, I have 4 children and myself went naked all winter and sure hope some way can be fixed [so] we can get some clothes to wear."[12] Etia Glen wrote from Forrest City, Arkansas, complaining, "now a few of us are in real need of clothing."[13] She wrote about herself and her husband, plus another man, Charlie Rodgers. She insisted that the union had to help them because they had each produced cotton that year. She believed that because they had worked, and worked hard, that they deserved to have their basic needs met.

The 1934 Memphis socialists' survey found that many sharecroppers and tenant farmers were also being evicted from their houses and land. They speculated that evictions were occurring because the landlords wanted a larger share of parity money from the Agricultural Adjustment Administration. As more and more people were made homeless, they turned to the STFU for help. William H. Stultz reported desperately to the Union that he, his wife, and their six children were "destitute" on the highways in Cross County, Arkansas. They had no home, no money, no property, and no secure work. Stultz reported that he had first been evicted from his home on a plantation near Parkin, Arkansas, in February 1934, in the dead of winter, and he and his family had wandered from place to place for over a year desperately trying to find lodging.[14]

Henry Peters, head of the Wynne, Arkansas, local, told Mitchell that ten families had asked him to find them houses for the winter. Peters reported that families were "well perpard for food the jess want help fare out of the weather."[15] Clayton Thompson wrote that thirty-two families had been "put off the Chapman Dewey place" and wanted to know if the union could help them find new places to live.[16] Hays Perry reported to the union that after his wife died he had been "put off" the Bunch place near Roundpound, Arkansas. Perry had not worked in his fields for a few days because he had gone to bury his wife. When he returned, he discovered to his horror that he had been evicted. In desperation he wrote to the union begging officials to "please tell me what to do as I dont no."[17] These requests were not the radical call for land distribution; instead, they were desperate pleas for immediate help. As word of the union spread, many desperate men and women hoped the STFU would be their salvation in this moment of profound crisis.

Immediate concerns about food, clothing, and a place to live were very important to sharecroppers and tenant farmers that joined the STFU. They also joined the union because their landlords were no longer providing traditional services. Though contracts differed from place to place, landlords typically promised to provide land, housing, fuel, tools, work stock, feed for the work stock, seed, and one-half the fertilizer. Tenants, in return, promised to provide labor and one-half the fertilizer. Crops would then be split between plantation owner and tenant based upon an agreed percentage. The percentage would be slightly different for sharecroppers who were legally only wage workers. Sharecroppers provided only labor and then took as wages an agreed upon crop percentage. Sharecroppers, like tenants, would be provided with "furnishings" either in the form of money or food that would then be deducted when, at season's end, it came time to settle accounts. [18] Usually landlords would repair houses and barns and make sure their tenants had a doctor. With the cataclysmic changes occurring in the agricultural South in the 1930s, however, landlords found it less in their interests to take care of sharecroppers and tenants. One sharecropper complained that the "landlord haven't fixed the barn yet nor have he fixed the house just might as well be living out of doors."[19] Another cropper complained from Marked Tree, Arkansas, that when he was sick his landlord "would not pay my doctor bill."[20] In desperation she wrote, "I am tired [of] working for nothin it is worser now than it was [under] slavery—the[y] woad give us close an food but know thy just give us a hard way to go."[21] As the plantation system died, services that landlords had traditionally provided also died. To many sharecroppers and tenant farmers this change was completely unacceptable, and they wanted the Union to fight for these services, which they felt were their rights.

Another major reason sharecroppers and tenant farmers joined the STFU was to get government money that had been promised them by Agricultural Adjustment contracts. One local leader wrote that his members had gone to collect their money. Each member was ushered into a dark room where the owner sat at a table between two of his riders who had guns in their belts. The tenants were given the option of leaving the land or signing over their government money to the landowner. The STFU leader cried, "we dident get justers."[22] A member wrote from Altheimer, Arkansas, in 1937, to tell how his landlord had stolen his money by having him sign a contract turning over his parity check. He wanted the check placed in his hand and not that of his landlords.[23] Other sharecroppers and tenant farmers wrote with the same complaint and demands. Ansley Garrett wrote, "Dear Secretary, these few lines to let you here from local 104. Lisen, 12 men hir on Mr. Linzie Bringforth place, Duneyhue Plantation, south of road 50 and Black Fish binge, lisen, we 12 men have never got but 1 paritie, no plow up money, no rental payment 1935. Paritie has not come yet, so he say. Let me here from you at once, can we get this money?"[24] Abe Glenn wrote from Turrell, Arkansas, to complain that he had not yet received his parity check for 1935 and wanted the union to help him. In complete outrage he declared, "It is unjust."[25]

Sharecroppers and tenant farmers by definition walked that thin line between just barely making ends meet and starvation. Not receiving money for a season's work was cataclysmic. In many of their letters when sharecroppers and tenant farmers talked of money they spoke about the injustice of their situation. By justice most did not mean equal distribution of land or the even control of the surplus value of the crop. They had in mind the more pragmatic goal of the timely distribution of the money that was rightfully theirs as sharecroppers and tenants under the New Deal plan.

Throughout the 1930s landowners began to replace sharecroppers and tenant farmers with day laborers. Day laborers worked for much lower wages and did not require the furnishings provided to sharecroppers and tenant farmers. The landlord also had no legal obligation to provide laborers houses or services. Day laborers were simply wage-hands without claim to a portion of the crop. Many sharecroppers and tenant farmers saw the trend toward day laborers as a serious threat to their security and wanted to use the union to take action. In August 1937, for example, the Earle, Arkansas, local claimed that planters in the area had made a deal to transport day laborers from Tennessee by railroad. The local, "Circulat[ed] a petition to the govenor of Arkansas to see if he can stop the labor from coming out of Tennessee in to Arkansas forcing our labor here at Earle to work for nothing or starve to death."[26] Two weeks later the same local wrote back to Mitchell calling for a strike to stop the influx of day laborers.[27] Echoing the same concerns,

Earl Hollis was concerned about planters who were bringing in Mexican cotton pickers to replace sharecroppers and tenant farmers.[28]

Of all the reasons that men and women joined the STFU the primary motivating force seems to have been concerns about the availability of land. This concern took two forms. Sharecroppers and tenant farmers were concerned with finding land to work the following year. And, they were concerned about their long-term desire to own and farm their own land.

Short-term desire for land may seem strange: why would people want to stay in an obviously oppressive system? But the letters in union files suggest that many sharecroppers and tenant farmers who joined the STFU were bound to this system by habit and by memory and were not willing to give it up to go into wage labor.

Nelson Parker wrote Mitchell from Earle, Arkansas, saying that he and his wife were "ragady and hungry" because they had not had any land to farm in 1935. Parker had tried to find day labor but such work was hard to secure because of the massive competition in his area. He was having to depend on his twenty-five-year-old daughter, a schoolteacher, to provide money for his family, but recently she had lost her position. Parker requested that the Union help him get land to sharecrop in 1936.[29] Elizabeth Pettigrue of Wabbaseka, Arkansas, was the head of a women's local. She was concerned about a number of needy families in her area who had not produced a crop and could not get land on which to grow one. She wanted to know if the union would "please tell me how to go about [finding them land]."[30]

Many sharecroppers and tenant farmers were concerned with a more long-term issue. The dream of land ownership had a long history in both southern black and white cultures. From the earliest days of emancipation, freed people expressed a desire to own land. As Roger Ransom and Richard Sutch point out, "In an agricultural society the possession of land [was] the key to affluence, the source of economic security, and the basis of an estate to be passed on to one's children."[31] The former enslaved people offered a number of reasons why they had the right to land ownership. Some believed that land ownership would complete their independence; others believed that land was the birthright of those who had worked; still others believed that they had a divine right to land ownership; and others argued that they had made the ultimate sacrifice to save the nation by fighting in the Union army and should be rewarded with land ownership.[32] Many former slaves shared the sentiments of Reverend Garrison Frazier when he spoke to General Sherman and Secretary of War Stanton in 1864, "The way we can best take care of ourselves is to have land, and turn it and till it by our own labor. . . ."[33]

Like former enslaved people, nineteenth-century white farmers had learned from an early age to respect, work, and own land. From the Republic's earliest days an ideology had existed that gave land ownership divine sanction. Thomas Jefferson claimed that "those who labor in the earth are the chosen people of God. . . ."[34] Steven Hahn, in his study of white yeomen farmers in Georgia, found that this ideology persisted through the antebellum period. Yeomen farmers, Hahn demonstrated, held to a republican ideology in which freedom, independence, and self-sufficiency were all tied to landownership.[35] Thus, both white and black farmers had a long-term commitment to that ideal. Both believed that a life of independence and self-sufficiency was the only way to live with honor and dignity, and both believed that this life was tied to land ownership.

In the 1930s these ideas were to be found in the worldviews of men and women, both black and white, who joined the STFU. Although sharecroppers and tenant farmers were mainly concerned with how they were going to survive from day to day, they also wanted to be sure they would always be able to support themselves and their families. The Marked Tree, Arkansas, local passed a resolution in 1935 stating, "We want jobs—not charity. We are willing to work we want work."[36] Andrew Ice wanted land so he and his family could "have things like other people."[37] Chester Wright wrote to Mitchell from Dixie, Arkansas, in the fall of 1935, wanting to know about the "land problem." He reported, "We is goin to need a Home." He wanted the union to do all it could to help him find a place to live.[38] While asking for more membership books for new sharecroppers that were joining his local, Austin Williams also wrote asking Mitchell for land. Williams reported that he had lived on the same farm for eight years, but his landlord was now trying to evict him. In a postscript to his letter, Williams stated that he was trying to get a "place to farm" and "want[ed] to rent or bye from the government and if you can help me out pease do so."[39]

Another sharecropper, J. W. Washington, wrote to Mitchell in late 1935 from Earle, Arkansas, looking for "justice." He had worked for years as a "shear worker" struggling to "try to start [himself] with out mules and tools." He reported that he could not make it on his own, and wanted the union to supply him with land, mules, and tools. Because his wife was sick he wanted to "get placed as early as I can. . . ."[40]

In 1935 the union also sent out its first questionnaire attempting to discover the rank and file's desires on the land issue. Union leaders had been in contact with government officials who were trying to solve the farming crisis and wanted input from sharecroppers and tenant farmers. Rank and file members were instructed to examine four potential plans, and choose the ones they liked "best and second best." The first plan would have continued the sharecropping and tenant farming system with the government as landlord. The second plan would have made the government landowner, with tenants and sharecroppers renting from it. Under this plan the government would have made available low-interest, long-term loans to help tenants between payments. Each person would work for himself under the government's supervision and would own any improvements made to the land. The third plan called for cooperative farming. Machinery, land, and crops would have been owned collectively by the people, with profits divided according to the proportion of work done by each family. A family would also have been given a garden plot of its own. The fourth plan called for individual land ownership. Farmers would have been given a piece of land large enough to support their family, financed by a twenty or thirty-year mortgage which they would then have repaid to the government. This plan, in the words of the questionnaire, was "every man for himself."[41]

Results of this questionnaire are revealing. Sharecroppers and tenant farmers overwhelmingly supported plans two and four. Plan four, individual land ownership, received fifty-eight percent of "first choice" votes, and twenty-five percent of "second choice" votes. Plan two, government ownership, received nineteen percent of "first choice" votes and sixty-seven percent of "second choice" votes. These two plans offered sharecropper and tenant farmers the greatest autonomy. Plan four would have taken tenants out of the sharecropping and tenant farming system and placed them on their own farms, where they could prove themselves. Plan two would have moved sharecroppers and tenant farmers up in the tenant system to the higher position of renter. This plan would have moved these families out from under landowners whom most felt to be dishonest and evil. Under this plan, sharecroppers and tenant farmers would also have had more control over any improvements they might make to the land.

Overwhelming losers in this survey were plans one and three. Plan one, continuing the system as it was under government ownership, received six percent of the "first choice" votes, and one percent of the "second choice" votes. Plan three, the cooperative farming system, received sixteen percent of the "first choice" votes, and five percent of the "second choice" votes. Plan one began with the words "Continue the present sharecropping and tenant plans." This was probably enough for those involved in the "present system" to vote against it. Sharecroppers and tenant farmers also voted against plan three, which was the plan that Union leaders, who were Socialist Party members, promoted. In this survey, rank and file sharecroppers and tenant farmers decidedly sided with private ownership and autonomous living, reaffirming their long-held belief in the dignity of individual landownership. In contrast to positions held at the time and to positions held by some historians today, sharecroppers and tenant farmers were willing to work and support their families if they were just given a chance.

In early 1936 a rumor floated around the Arkansas delta that the government had taken over the Twist Plantation, one of the largest Arkansas farms. The rumor turned out to be false, but some sharecroppers and tenant farmers became so excited by this news that they wrote, wanting a piece of the land. William Johnson wrote excitedly to J. R. Butler, at the time president of the Union, on behalf of himself and two other sharecroppers, when he had heard that the government had placed land under control of the STFU. Johnson wanted to arrange to place the three of them on land as quickly as possible.[42]

The vast majority of sharecroppers and tenant farmers had farmed all their lives. Many of these men and women loved farming and only wanted to move up the agricultural ladder. W. G. Wellshad signed a three-year contract on a farm but was evicted in 1937. When he turned to the WPA he found that the agency would not or could not give him a job. He wrote, "I feel like I am in title to sum Relief bad as iny body in the world." He loved his work and wanted the union to know that he would be the "prodest man on arth[earth] if I could only get good little hom by the government on a long time pay. I be happy and work hard."[43] George Bostick wrote from Gilmore, Arkansas, that he had been a sharecropper but now had no job. He wanted the union to help him get land because he was getting old and "did love to farm."[44]

In 1937, Lula Parchman wrote to H. L. Mitchell, to explain her situation. She had been farming on the J. H. Blunt Plantation since 1933, and in a period when there was no work to be done on the plantation she planted a corn crop in a vacant lot across from her house. Wesley Jackson, plantation boss on the Blunt Plantation, plowed up the corn because he wanted to rent the lot to someone else. In the midst of this she exclaimed, "They don't regard my rights at all."[45] The word "rights" in this exclamation obviously referred to the right to farm, unmolested by a landlord. She then went on to say, "I want only a chance to make my own living and not the other get the profit of my labor and I suffer. The chance to live independent I don't want what belong to others. I only want the portion due me for comfort."[46] Here in the most direct language possible, Parchman affirmed her desire to live an independent life. She did not want more than was hers. She considered her long-time labor on the land to be a badge of her right to own land. Someone, the Union or government, she believed, owed her justice. And justice was land that she could call her own.

Irvine Nickerson wrote in 1939 that she too wanted a resettlement home where "we can work and make a living and be from under Old Boss. We don't want relief we want to work and make our own living." She wanted freedom. She did not want to work for "Old Boss." She wanted to be like "Old Boss"—free to support her family on her own land.[47]

The union leader's response to these sometimes-desperate pleas for help mostly went unheeded. H. L. Mitchell and the other men and women who ran the national STFU office were not callused people; they simply did not have the financial or ideological resources to help thousands of rank and file members. Ideologically, most of the socialist leadership did not share the sharecroppers and tenant farmers' desire to own their own land. Financially, as Mitchell often said, the union was "an organization of poor people . . . trying to better . . . conditions . . . the union has no money."[48] J. R. Butler once wrote to an organizer telling him "money in the union is as scarce as hen's teeth." Most rank and file members soon realized they would receive little financial help from the national office. They would have to depend on one another in their locals.

Although men and women joined the STFU out of a multitude of specific economic needs and grievances, there was one continuous thread in their letters: the desire to make sure they and their families were secure.[49] Whether security meant trying to get food and clothing or a place to live, making sure that their boss provided the traditional services they had grown to expect, fighting for their rightful share of the government money, fighting day laborers who they believed were stealing their work, or trying to get land, the overriding concern of these men and women was the security of their families and their neighbors.

This familial concern was not simply rooted in the secular ideology of American values of landownership. It was rooted in what Howard Kester, a socialist minister who worked with the STFU, would describe as a "fundamentalist" Christian worldview.[50] To understand why these men and women joined the Union, we must understand the ideology they brought with them to the union.

In studying the values and worldview of sharecroppers and tenant farmers there are certain limits to what historians can know. Sharecroppers and tenant farmers made statements from which we can attempt to draw out their values and worldview; they did not articulate a systematic philosophy. The historian is therefore limited, but from their letters we can see something of the culture they brought to the union and how that culture shaped their struggles. The sharecroppers and tenant farmers brought to the STFU a deeply held commitment to a rural, fundamentalist, and Pentecostal Protestantism. Although they were Baptist, Methodist, Holiness, or Pentecostal, they held to certain core beliefs which they drew upon to create not only the way in which they viewed everyday events in their lives, but also to form and fashion the STFU. This worldview called upon union members to analyze their situation in the light of scriptures, to fight against injustice, and to care for one another. These rank and file values often contrasted to the secular worldview of union leaders such as H. L. Mitchell, but it also sometimes contradicted the social gospel ideas held by union leaders such as Howard Kester, Claude Williams, and Ward Rogers. Historians Anthony Dunbar and Robert F. Martin have analyzed union leaders who held to the social gospel ideas. Alva Taylor had trained these ministers at Vanderbilt University in the 1920s and early 1930s. The economic suffering they saw in their local parishes and their involvement in the labor movement led these ministers towards a radical position. Their brand of Christianity taught that capitalism was at an end and that capitalists lacked the motivation and will to help make a better world. Therefore, capitalism needed to be abolished. God's avenue for changing the world was going to be the Communist or Socialist Parties.[51]

In contrast to the secular or social gospel worldviews of their leaders, sharecroppers and tenant farmers brought with them values that arose from a deep and abiding religious faith, which was reflected in the everyday use of religious language, symbols, and stories. Religion, for these men and women, was not a theoretical construction, nor was it abstracted from their daily lives. For sharecroppers and tenant farmers, Jesus was as real as the plow they followed down the rows. Evangelical Christianity dominated the South.[52] Divisions did exist, of course. Some were Methodists, others Baptist, and there were even a few Presbyterians. Holiness and Pentecostal churches competed with the Assemblies of God and Christian Churches, but these divisions, which were real, do not completely explain the South.[53] In rural areas, where STFU members lived, there tended to be fewer churches than one would find in cities. The reason for this was simple. Most denominations required the local congregation to raise money to sustain a preacher or maintain a building. Because sharecroppers and tenant farmers did not, as a rule, have money, they usually had to rely upon traveling ministers. Rural churches typically met only once a month. As a result, a Baptist might attend a Methodist service one Sunday and a Holiness meeting the next. Ida Davis was a Methodist who regularly attended Holiness, Baptist, and Assembly of God services.[54] Men and women who wrote the STFU drew upon their Bible as their key to understating the STFU and to provide answers to the problems facing them.[55]

It was a religious worldview that the sharecroppers and tenant farmers brought with them to the STFU. It was this Bible based worldview that they drew upon to fight against planters.[56] To any observer in our moment of history or in the midst of the 1930s it is almost impossible to view the sharecropping and tenant farming system as anything but an extremely hopeless situation. But one senses in the letters of sharecroppers and tenant farmers the absolute confidence that they felt. They somehow knew they were going to overcome their situation.

Religion was the prism through which these men and women saw the world around them. It was how they saw and made sense of the events that occurred. When they needed places to have their meetings, they called upon local churches to open their buildings. In their local and national meetings, they began with prayer, bible readings, and hymns and gospel songs. They referred to each other with the New Testament titles of "brother" and "sister."[57] All called for the "Lord's" presence to be in their midst. They lived in a world submerged in the supernatural; yet, their world was not one of spiritual idealism and apathy towards the world around them. They saw no discontinuity between the supernatural and natural reality. What occurred in one realm affected the other.[58]

The names of their locals also showed signs of their commitment to this religious worldview. They chose names that communicated to a mostly illiterate populace stories from both the Old Testament and New. These local manes drew on deep and old Biblical symbols. The "Shiloh local" reminded them when all the assembly of the Hebrew people congregated around Joshua after Yahweh had "subdued the land before them." It was there the Hebrews established Yahweh's tabernacle. For these sharecroppers and tenant farmers the sacredness of the local was communicated in its name.[59]

The "New Bethal local" told the story of Jacob's dream in which Jacob declared, "Surely the Lord is in this place." The presence of the supernatural was as real to them as the ground they walked on. Many other locals used Biblical names to communicate commitment to their religious values.[60]

From this religious worldview, the sharecroppers and tenant farmers of the STFU attempted to change their world. While many like Lula McDonald used prayer as their political tool to change the world, others chose to use their faith to struggle more aggressively.[61]

In January 1936, J. W. Washington wrote to H. L. Mitchell to inquire about membership books he had requested. He also reported that the previous Friday at his local's monthly meeting a group of planters and their overseers had broken into their meeting and beaten and shot at some of their members. He said the trouble began when "we had just begun to get in the mids of a big time." They had started the meeting, in the normal fashion, with songs. In the midst of describing the euphoria that swept the meeting when they sang "I shall not be moved," Washington said, "That song I do believe sprung from our lips with the music of God. It [rolled] my mind back to the time when Moses was leading the children of Irsell."[62] It is unknown whether Washington was black or white, but in both African-American and rural white churches, the Moses story was of primary importance. Not only was God present with his people, but it seemed that he was there to lead them. This was a powerful weapon with which to explain their beatings and shootings.

A. T. Williams saw Mitchell as Moses. Williams compared Mitchell's suffering to that of the Hebrew patriarch, but he hopefully declared that just as Moses was called by God to liberate the Hebrews, he believed that Mitchell was called by God to liberate sharecroppers and tenant farmers. This biblical image gave sharecroppers and tenant farmers hope in the midst of darkness and despair.[63]

The majority of sharecroppers and tenant farmers who wrote the union refused to see their religion as an abstract construct. Instead they saw it as something that had to be used. Sometime in late 1937 or early 1938, Rebecca Cline wrote to the union with a brief statement of her core values. She began by telling union leaders that the "peril of Religion" is "that we shall think of religion as a matter of merely of saving our own souls." She believed that this narrow view of religion made the soul wanting to be saved absolutely worthless. After speaking out against unused religion, Cline then said, "You recall the story of Jesus used of the poor man who had been beaten and robbed." Then she added, "The priest and Levite came along and passed by on the other side. They were merely trying to play safe. Let some one else help the poor man and furnish the money necessary to care for him. Jesus told the story because that was the current Idea of religion at that day."[64]

We do not know what led her to tell this story, although it is known that many city churches worked with planters to keep sharecroppers and tenant farmers out of the STFU. She may well have been responding to one of these churches. It is interesting that she does not finish the story as it is told in the Gospels. In the Gospels, the Good Samaritan comes along the road and gives aid to his sworn enemy, the Hebrew. Instead of telling this part of the story, Cline began to tell the union leaders that she and her local were doing all they could to raise money for the poor. It seems, although we cannot be sure, that she saw herself and her local as the Good Samaritan. Religious people around her were the "priests and Levite," but here was a group of poor men and women doing what they believed Jesus had told them to do, taking care of one another. Cline's story reveals two things: it shows the way in which the religious culture in which these people were submerged was used to justify and solidify union support. This story also shows how the religious culture filled sharecroppers and tenant farmers with confidence.[65]

In 1938 the members of Local 11 decided they had to get the attention of someone in power or their situation would never change. So they enlisted their local president, Henry Peters, to write a letter on their behalf to U.S. Senator Hattie Carraway. The letter began by asking Carraway to consider the sharecroppers' condition. Peters told Carraway that many of their members were on the side of the highway without food or shelter, and he blamed this condition upon selfish and greedy planters who did not care what happened to the poor. Asking Carraway to first read the third chapter of Malachi and the fifth chapter of James, Peters appealed to her to help the poor and to convince the farmers in Cross County to help.

Malachi 3 and James 5 both address the rich and powerful's responsibility to the poor and to workers. Malachi 3.2–5 reads in part, "But who may abide the day of his coming? And who shall stand when he appeareth? For he is like a refiners fire . . . And I will come near to you to judgment, and I will be a swift witness against . . . those that oppress the hireling in his wages. . . ." And James 5.1–6 reads,

> Go to now, ye rich men, weep and howl for your miseries that shall come upon you. Your riches are corrupted, and your garments are moth-eaten. Your gold and silver is cankered; and the rust of them shall be a witness against you, and shall eat your flesh as it were fire. Ye have heaped treasure together for the last days. Behold, the hire of the laborers who have reaped down your

> fields, which is of you kept back by fraud, crieth: and the cries of them which have reaped are entered into the ears of the Lord of Sabaoth. Ye have lived in pleasure on the Earth, and been wanton; ye have nourished your hearts, as in the day of slaughter. Ye have condemned and killed the just; and he doth not resist you.

Sharecroppers and tenant farmers in this local were using religion in two ways. They were looking at their world and critiquing the oppression they experienced through their god's eyes. In these verses their god was telling them that he hates oppression of poor laboring people. Sharecroppers and tenant farmers latched onto this analysis and used it to understand their world. But, they were also using these verses to warn Carraway. She represented the rich and powerful, and if she did not consider the poor she would be condemned on the "day of his coming." Sharecroppers and tenant farmers were sincere in their belief that vengeance was God's, and they believed that if Carraway did not help them she would be damned. This empowered them again in two ways. It told them that they were on the right side and at the end of history they would win. But, it also allowed them to pressure Carraway and the planters, to shame them into helping sharecroppers and tenant farmers. Since landowners and politicians came from the same religious world as sharecroppers and tenant farmers, they probably would not want to be thought of, nor have to think of themselves, as less then firmly committed to God's word.

Sharecroppers and tenant farmers' religious worldview also shaped their analysis of the change going on around them. It allowed them to have a powerful and persuasive vocabulary to try and shame leaders of their country into helping. It also motivated them to help one another. Although modern social analysts might argue that community charity was never enough when people were facing structural injustice, to sharecroppers and tenant farmers the religious values they brought with them to the STFU taught them that the battle on the temporal sphere had to be fought on two fronts: they had to stand against evil people who were trying to destroy them and their families; but more importantly, they had to take care of one another. In one of the most amazing documents in the STFU's files, a play written by one of the rank and file, communicated this sense of community with passion and conviction.

Flotine Hodge lived in Morton, Arkansas. She was a rank and file member who sat down and wrote a play that she hoped would be acted out in all STFU's locals. Hodge was attempting to get people to join the union and to stay committed. In that regard the play was obviously a propaganda piece. Its story makes the union seem larger than it really was. The play had neighbors "wearing slightly better clothes because they were union members," while the non-union members were "poorly clothed." In the play, entitled "Southern Tenant Farmers' Union Forever," John and Mary Jones are sharecroppers on the Smith Plantation. John and Mary have a young son named Johnnie who is sick with tuberculosis and may die if he does not soon get healthy food and a doctor's care. John goes to Mr. Smith, the plantation owner, expecting him to act like a decent man and help those in his community. John asks for money to get a doctor and groceries, but Mr. Smith is a selfish man who will not help John. Smith tells John that if he helped him he would have to help everyone on his place. The conflict is clear-cut in the writer's mind. The sharecroppers and tenant farmers expect the rich man to do his Christian duty and help his neighbors, but Mr. Smith rejects the role. The Jones's neighbors, Jess and Elizabeth Taylor, are STFU members and have attempted to persuade the Jones' to join the union. But Mary is scared and will not allow John to join. The Jones family eventually joins the Union when the Union leader brings the doctor and food to little Johnnie.

> MARY: I see now where I was wrong. We'll have money now to buy Johnnie medicine and the kind of food he needs. I sure do thank you all for this help. Maybe Johnnie will pull through now. (Wipes eye)
>
> JIMMIE: Don't thank us. Thank the Southern Tenant Farmers' Union. It was the Union that made it possible.
>
> JOHN (Goes to Mary and lays arm on shoulder): You see Mary. You see.
>
> MARY: Yes I do and I am going to join that Union.

(They face the audience and say together)

MARY AND JOHN: The Southern Tenant Farmers' Union, forever![66]

The theological message was as clear as the union propaganda. The Christian values that sharecroppers and tenant farmers held most dear were no longer found in the rich and mighty but instead in the lowly membership of the STFU. We do not know how men and women responded to this message, but it must have provoked a powerful response among people who shared a common set of assumptions about Christian obligations to help the poor.

Men and women who joined the STFU did not abandon their culture when the entered the union. Although H. L. Mitchell and Clay East brought atheism to the union in hopes of enlightening the ignorant masses, and men like Howard Kester would introduce social gospel ideas to the rank and file, these ideas never dominated the way sharecroppers and tenant farmers thought. Sharecroppers and tenant farmers brought their faith into the union and developed a movement culture. This movement culture acted in four ways within the union. It gave them a sense of confidence by assuring them that good would triumph over evil. It allowed them to place the changes going on around them into a moral framework and see such events as a conflict between good and evil. It provided them language to condemn the evil they saw around them and to fight back. And finally, it gave them a strong sense of community and responsibility for one another.

No one better exemplifies the reasons why men and women joined the STFU and how they used their culture to work within the Union than Stephen Seys.[67] Although Seys lived outside the delta, he is still typical of how the majority of rank and file thought. He resided in a county high in the Ozark Mountains. In the seven letters retained in the STFU files, Seys revealed himself to be a man with strongly held opinions. He seemed to be a lonely man who would write long detailed letters about his struggle to make his part of the world better.

Stephen Seys was born and raised in Zion, Illinois, "a little town between Chicago, Ill. and Milwaukee, Wis." Although he does not explain why he left Zion, by July, 1933 he had left home and hit the road. Seys joined that growing group of Americans wandering around the countryside looking for a way to support themselves and their families. Seys ended up in Tennessee, where he worked for the Tennessee Valley Authority on dams, as a contractor for cement work. From Tennessee, Seys moved to Arkansas, where in Pine Bluff he first worked for Senator Joseph Robinson's company laying sewers. When the job ended in November 1934, Seys moved to North Little Rock, where he got a job "cutting cord wood for Justen Mathews . . . for 50 cents per cord." In North Little Rock he lived in a "Hoo Boo jungle" that had been set up in the woods. He slept on the ground and cooked his food in tin cans, owning only a shirt, shoes and a pair of overhauls.

Finally, Seys settled in the little mountain town in Jasper, the county seat of Newton County, Arkansas. When Seys arrived in Jasper he went to work for Fred Palmore. Seys worked for his room and board, clearing lumber off land Palmore owned. According to Seys, Palmore offered him four acres of land for personal use and a mule if Seys would clear the land. Seys cleared the land but Palmore took back half of the four acres and never allowed Seys to use the mule. Seys would not be stopped, however, and he got seeds from his "folks in Ill.—NC—and Texas" and raised a garden. Seys quit Palmores' farm when the owner would not let him work his garden on Sundays, telling Seys, "If any crop work is done on Sundays it would be done on my crops!!!!"

Seys went to work next for C. W. Twyman, the "Newton County cow king." He worked for board and two dollars a week. When he quit Twyman's place, he went to work for Austin J. Harrison, laboring for seventy-five cents per day. He was promised an eight- or nine-hour day. But two weeks after he started, Harrison had Seys working from daybreak until one hour after dark for fifty cents a day. Seys said that he lived on "garden stuff—sepperrated goats milk and cow feed cooked in a mush." In the midst of this, with the help of his mother, Seys made enough money to put down a payment on eighty acres of land. He had no cabin to live in, so on his first night he made a log fire which he slept by for days until he built a "split shingle roof."

Seys did not explain how he heard of the Southern Tenant Farmers Union, but he did say that the government relief agent in Jasper, Alvin Phillips, told him that he was "not supposed to get ahead . . . only supposed to get by." By 1936, Seys had secured a charter for local number 203 and was the chief STFU organizer for Newton County.[68]

Like all union organizers Seys encountered antiunion feelings: "some feel that it [the union] is the mark of the beast—and some do not want to join a gang of outlaws. . . ."[69] A man Seys calls Uncle John Waters promised to take him around Newton County to introduce him to people. Waters had sold nursery stock in the county for over forty years and was well known and respected. Even with this influential man's backing, the leaders of the county still threatened to kill Seys. One day when he went to pick up his mail, the postmaster and another man were talking about a railroad strike near Harrison where the union leaders had been hung. The postmaster asked Seys, "how I would like to be strung up like they did the RR union heads in Harrison?"[70]

Seys had been given permission by J. R. Butler, the president of the Southern Tenant Farmers Union, to organize lumber workers as well as sharecroppers. He would set out to organize with his pack mule, his fishing pole and all of the labor newspapers he could carry. In describing the conditions of the people working part time in lumber, he reported: The living conditions are much worse in the US. Forest where timber companies have bought up cheap timber and labor fines himself dependent on and at the merce of Mr. Timber King.[71] Again Seys reported,

> What do we find—a tippicle Hoo Boo Jungle—anything for shelter old tin sign boards—mill waist slabs—old roten canvas poles—the men have not time to split shingles and build the hill folks style cabins—here are the children without schools of any kind—women give berth to their babys in no more or less than Hoo Boo Jungle camps—improvised shelter—their hill billy homes are gone—they must work for what ever the timber company is willing to pay—buy from the timber companies commasarry—the mountain stores are gone.[72]

Seys blamed such misery upon New Deal programs. The New Deal relief agency in the county was controlled by one of the mill owners, Alvin Phillips, who was also the brother-in-law of Austin Harrison, one of the wealthiest landowners in Newton County. Seys reported with anger, "Yes there are those how have made lots of money by the New Deal," but the "farm and timber labor of all kinds are worse off then before the New Deal."[73]

Though he believed the New Deal was to blame for the poor's hardships, Seys joined the Union for two reasons: he wanted to farm and to not have to be dependent on any other person, and he wanted everyone to have the chance to get land. Seys had some amazing dreams for a man of his education. He dreamed of a fairer, more productive way of farming. He had been reading a book on Japanese farm methods and wanted to write a book on "a new and better hill farming."[74] He had learned that the "tipical Japaness farm is a 2 acre mountain side—stone wall terraced—here he raises all that he eats—not a cash crop to sell as Dixes King Cotton—these Japs takes 3 dayly papers—electricke lighty and 4 pool bathes a day and after super feels good anuf to write apoem and hang in the cherry tree."[75] Seys wanted farmers to plant trees as a cash crop. He also wanted each farm to be self-sufficient: "we should as far as we can raise on each farm everything we can that is used on that farm."[76] There was an obvious idealism in such a notion, but mixed with this was nostalgia for a way of farming he saw in the "golden past." "Yes go back 100 years or more in our ideals—raise what we use and use what we raise as far as we can but with new and better methods."[77]

Stephen Seys' world was rooted in Christianity, the result of influence by a Methodist pastor. The pastor began one of his Easter sermons with the words, "The grate multitudes of people are labor and the minority is those how do not have to work and we find our Lord on this particular location talking to a group of perhaps all the labor class."[78] Identifying Jesus with the laboring class it helped reaffirm that Jesus, who they believed to be God, was truly on their side, and it gave them real confidence. The Lord was on their side, and as Seys said, all the laborers were "God's children—'the least of these."[79] Because of the sharecroppers' religion there was hope, and in the end they had the assurance that they would win the battle before them. He used the Bible to organize, quoting a verse that said, "He how [*sic*] providest not for his own is worse than an infadal."[80]

Because of his religion, Seys expected people to be concerned about their neighbor and to care for one another in the community. The "culture of community" was a way of life, a mindset that stood in opposition to what Christopher Lasch identifies as the modern "culture of Narcissism."

Seys felt a strong responsibility for the people around him. He was deeply moved by the plight of timber workers. And he blamed the New Deal for the loss of community:

> The US [government] has did away with the little hillbilly schools and churches—the mountain store—the community—then she [the government] sells this timber for less—far less than it costs to raise timber. . . .[81]
>
> Because of this loss of community and the growing dependence of people on large land owners, government agencies, and timber companies, "there are those with no land and no work—no relief—no food no feed and no seeds!!!!!!!!"[82]

Seys was outraged by what he saw as the lack of compassion by relief agency head Alvin Phillips. When Seys was told that he could not receive aid because he was a single man, he responded with anger and remorse: "If that is true why is it that Joe Dee Morgan an old man and his wife and boy can not and has not got relief???!!WHY??!"[83] Seys also sought help for John Holt, who had been a strong timber worker with a wife and a number of small children. He was diagnosed with cancer and began a slow and painful death. Seys attempted to get him aid, but was unsuccessful. When Holt died, Seys and other union members made him a casket, and buried him "under a red ceder in a grave yard on a hill below the mountain and above the river."[84] It is obvious that Seys loved humanity and was totally confounded by the changes going on around him.

Seys appeared in the STFU letters suddenly in 1935. Just as suddenly he disappeared in 1938. He ended one of his letters by saying "something should be done . . ."[85] This summarized his view of life, as well as that of the vast majority of the STFU's rank and file. Something had to be done.

CHAPTER FIVE

HENDERSON BENTLY, SECRETARY OF the Poinsett County, Southern Tenant Farmers' Union local, was one of the earliest members to join the Union from the Norcross Plantation. Bently wrote in desperation to Union president J. R. Butler in 1937, wanting the Union to know that he had always been faithful, had diligently followed union leadership, and even went on strike when he knew it would cost him his home and livelihood. He wrote that he was evicted because of his union membership and had a "hard way to go." Bently wrote in despair that he had not farmed since 1934 when he had joined the union. And on that cold February morning he expressed pained disbelief that his interests were not being looked after by the union and suggested that non-union men had an easier life than he and his family. He wrote, "I have roat to the govenor for some place [even] if it in the woods so I can make me a livin I am tied trying to work by the day from sun up tell sun down for 75 cents I want to crop. So I will hafter stop looking to the union far help far I see it is now I am worst shape and them whoo ant union for they don't be evicted on the count of the Union no help from the union it two bad."[1]

In 1937, only three years after it began, many men and women like Henderson Bently began to leave the STFU. By 1938, the union's membership had fallen to 17,621, almost forty-nine percent below its 1937 high of 34,374. In two more years, it would plummet to 3000 members. By 1940, the union had lost ninety-one percent of its 1937 total.

Socialist activist Michael Harrington warned historians against seeing the Southern Tenant Farmers' Union as a "left-wing western in which the good guys always win."[2] The STFU was defeated. Arkansas landowners squashed the union as members attempted to stand for their rights.

The STFU's demise has been attributed to at least two external factors. Externally, the union faced the increased mechanization of cotton farming and tried to organize in the face of growing violence against its members. But as important as these two external factors were, the union's demise also can be attributed to two internal factors. The issue of race haunted the union from the earliest days. Would the union be integrated or would it be segregated? The tensions inherent in these questions would put strains on the union and help in its quick demise. Second, union leaders, although firmly committed to fulfilling the sharecroppers and tenant farmers' agenda, were ultimately unable to fulfil that agenda. We cannot be sure which of these factors, external or internal, were the most important. Sharecroppers rarely explained why they left the union, but those who did offer new possibilities for understanding the STFU's demise.

Using violence to control personal and social conflict had a long history in the nation, but especially in the South. The Old South's ruling class used duels as a common way to settle disputes, while the lower classes settled feuds with guns, fists, or knives. This violence did not abate after the Civil War. Historian Edward Ayers has remarked that the South had the highest late nineteenth century murder rate in the United States.[3] During Reconstruction the southern ruling class, as well as many poor whites who felt threatened by the rise of blacks to positions of power, reacted with violence, lynching, and murders. But as C. Vann Woodward points out, southern racial violence must be seen as part of the "general milieu of southern violence."[4] When the southern ruling class encountered a union of sharecroppers and tenant farmers, it drew upon this tradition of violence to attack the union's members and leaders.

Initially acts of violence were committed around the union's Marked Tree, Arkansas, headquarters. As early as November 1934, Mitchell reported the theft of his personal papers when his home had been broken into. Physical violence soon began. In March 1935 Arthur Brookings, an African-American preacher and a member of the union's Executive Council, reported that "night riders" came to his house and shot "hundreds" of bullets barely missing his family who were hiding under the bed. This act of terrorism forced him to flee his home in Marked Tree and go to Memphis.[5]

Union leaders were initially the targets of anti-union violence. Planters soon learned which of their sharecroppers and tenant farmers were union members and began to use violence to intimidate them.[6]

In February 1935 Arkansas Governor J. Marion Futrell received an urgent telegram from Anna Damon, acting National Secretary for the International Labor Defense League. She reported to the governor that a reign of terror was underway in Arkansas. She reported that a STFU meeting in Cross County was broken up one Friday night. Thugs beat two men and made death threats to all. In the spring the "reign of terror intensified with night riders going from town to town looking for union meetings. Union leaders quickly packed up their belongings and fled Marked Tree for the relative safety of Memphis, Tennessee. Back in Arkansas the union was recommending that its members stop holding public meetings. But staying out of the public eye did not stop the violence. It seemed to come in waves too high and too hard for people to stand against. In early April, E. B. McKinney's house was shot up and two men sleeping inside were wounded. In Holly Grove, Arkansas, the "Colored Baptist Church," which was used for union meetings, was burned to the ground. Even non-union meetings were broken up. Nightriders shot up a prayer meeting in Birdsong, Arkansas. People were afraid to hold meetings at night.[7]

In September 1935, at cotton picking time, the STFU launched a strike, pulling all cotton pickers out of the fields. The union's goal in the strike was to get higher wages for cotton picking the following year. Hundreds, perhaps thousands, of sharecroppers and tenant farmers leaving their fields in protest caught landowners off guard. Not wanting to lose their valuable crops, most landowners agreed to wage increases. Union leaders did not portray the cotton pickers' work stoppage as a strike for their own land or for the right to farm cooperatively, but instead as fulfillment of an immediate need for "higher wages."[8] In 1935, the average sharecropper or tenant farmer was making 40 to 65 cents per hundred pounds of cotton picked. The Union went on strike to guarantee a dollar per hundred pounds of cotton picked. Landowners had believed for so long that sharecroppers and tenant farmers had lost their will to fight, that when they finally went on strike landowners were surprised. George Stith, a member of the STFU who later became an organizer, remembered that landowners were "scared to death." Although landowners would not sign a contract with the union, they began to make deals with individual sharecroppers and tenants.[9] Although the 1935 strike caught planters by surprise, the reign of terror initiated by planters intensified in the fall and winter.

J. E. Cameron wrote H. L. Mitchell in November 1935 to report that he had organized a meeting of his local in Heath, Arkansas. More than two hundred men and women showed up that night to join the union. In the middle of Cameron's speech extolling the union, three men drove up in two cars and began to curse and "abuse" the crowd. When the men reached Cameron they said to him, "What in the hell are you doing here you son of a bitch shut up or I'll knok your brains out you damn bastard."[10] Another tenant wrote from Widener, Arkansas, to tell Mitchell that his landlord was "trying to stell my life."[11]

In 1936 planters continued to use violence to intimidate the sharecroppers and tenant farmers. In early January Hez Redmond and George Fly, two Union members, were severely beaten with an axehandle by H. D. Terrance who was a riding boss on the H. F. Avery Plantation. On January 16, deputy sheriffs Everette Hood and J. D. Preacher raided a union meeting being held in the St. Peters Church near Earle, Arkansas. Hood came into the meeting with a shotgun, demanding that all the union members file out of the building. Jim Ball, who was watching the front door for the union against such an attack, attempted to take the gun from Hood. There is evidence that Ball was armed with a pistol or a shotgun. Ball was eventually arrested. He was tried on the charge of "Assault with intent to kill." The court convicted and gave him seven years, although the Arkansas Supreme Court eventually reduced his sentence to two years. Later that night, Hood and Preacher returned to the church and shot at a group of union members in the road, wounding two men. Willie Hurst witnessed the shooting, and masked men at the home of another union member later murdered him. Before the killing, the men attempted to force Hurst to sign a statement exonerating Preacher and Hood from any involvement in the Earle, Arkansas, affair.[12]

Other sharecroppers and tenant farmers found their whole worlds wrecked because of their affiliation with the STFU. Henry Craft of Procter,

Arkansas, found his family evicted from their plantation in February 1935 along with twenty-five other families. Threatening the families with guns, the bosses tried to get them to name other union members. Two older African-Americans received beatings with leather straps because it was believed they were members of the STFU.[13]

At cotton picking time in 1936 the union attempted to call another strike, but this time landowners were prepared. The STFU strike began in May; almost immediately landowners began to retaliate. In Crittenden County, landowners opened what union leaders called "Concentration Camps," arresting sharecroppers and tenant farmers and holding them in a stockade near Earle, Arkansas. The union charged that sharecroppers and tenant farmers were then forced to work in cotton fields at gunpoint. In September 1936, a federal grand jury indicted the deputy sheriff of Crittenden County, Paul Peacher, for "aiding and abetting in holding in slavery" a group of sharecroppers and tenant farmers who belonged to the STFU.[14] Despite the indictment, violence against white and black sharecroppers continued. That year C. A. Withers reported from Edmondson, Arkansas, that he had been threatened with flogging because he was in communication with the union. After a local landowner had discovered the presence of the union in Edmondson, the local postmistress reported to him every time a sharecropper or tenant farmer received a letter from the union.[15] Withers also reported that the local could not have meetings because members were afraid of additional violence from landowners. He wanted the union to help end this violence so that sharecroppers and tenant farmers could meet in peace.[16]

Deep within the memories of both those who supported the union and those who opposed were the events that occurred in Elaine, Arkansas, in 1919. On September 30, 1919, in a little town in Philips County, about three miles north of Elaine, a local chapter of the Progressive Farmers and Household Union (PFHUA) was attempting to meet in a Baptist church. The men and women who made up this union had hired a white Republican lawyer named O. S. Bratton to file lawsuits against landlords who failed to settle fairly. These sharecroppers and tenant farmers wanted to see the books the planters kept; they wanted to end the debt peonage that held them and their families in virtual slavery year to year. While the details of what happened on that September night are contested, it is certain that a white police officer was killed by an African-American. This act would start a race war in which hundreds of African-Americans were killed.[17] Union members and planters both recalled this event as a way to understand what the STFU was. After breaking up a meeting in Earle, Arkansas, in January 1936 the night riders told the crowd that they were going have another Elaine, "but this time both white and black would be slaughtered." Even Governor Futrell understood the union in terms of Elaine when he argued that "Negroes can be stimulated to the wildest outrages. The Elaine trouble is yet fresh in the minds of the people over here. They know that a Negro is a dangerous tool in the hands of an agitator." In June of that year the Reverend James Myers of the Federal Council of Churches reported that hostile crowds had shouted "Elaine, Elaine" at union meetings.[18]

If the planters were wanting to start another Elaine, the rank and file members of the Union, and sometimes even the leaders, were willing to use violence if pushed too far. Just like the men and women of Elaine, STFU members wanted to protect their lives and livelihoods. For years Mitchell attempted to portray another image. In a speech given in 1973 at Princeton University, Mitchell argued, "I often say that when Martin Luther King Jr. was a very small boy a group of black and white sharecroppers adopted the policy of nonviolence." But the reality was far more complex.[19]

There was always great fear among the leaders that the rank and file would return violence with violence. As the Ball case suggests, some union members were armed. In the summer of 1935, J. R. Butler, the union's president, was concerned that violence in Cross County was going to be met with violence. He was convinced that there was going to be a "pitched battle."[20] Into 1936, as the reign of terror increased, the union received a letter explaining that the sharecroppers and tenant farmers in Earle, Arkansas, had agreed to bring weapons to their next meeting and to defend themselves if again attacked by the planters. And J. L. Lynn of Trumann, Arkansas, wanted to "call the men to bullets."[21] Three union leaders also admitted to being willing to use violence. Nightriders confronted C. T. Carpenter, the Union's lawyer, many times because of his union work. One night in the spring of 1935 he met a group on his front porch carrying a shotgun. After that, whenever he left his home, it was necessary for him to carry his revolver. H. L. Mitchell and Clay East would later admit that even they carried pistols to protect themselves.[22]

The most fascinating example of violent rhetoric used by union members and appreciated by the rank and file is the bizarre tale of the trial of Ward Rodgers. In early 1935, the STFU had a meeting in Marked Tree to bring new members to the union. At the meeting the fiery young Methodist minister Ward Rodgers spoke. It was an exciting day. The leaders of the STFU had expected fifty or sixty people to show up, but instead 1,500 had come to the meeting. As Ward Rodgers finished his speech he asked if Mr. McKinney was in the auditorium. This would have been acceptable behavior if McKinney was a white man, but he was a black Baptist preacher. Rodgers had ignored a clear rule of the Jim Crow South—white men did not call black men "mister." When it was determined that McKinney had not arrived yet, Rodgers continued with his speech. In its climax, Rodgers shouted that he could "lead a lynch mob on every plantation owner in the county if I wanted to." The crowd went crazy; men threw their hats into the air and yelled in affirmation. To the law of Poinsett County this was the language of Elaine, and it could not be tolerated. While Mitchell spoke Rodgers was arrested. The crowd also excited Mitchell, and he made matters worse by telling the crowd that "the first son of a bitch that sticks his head in a pillow case will get the hell shot out of him." Mitchell escaped to Memphis before the local police could arrest him. Rodgers would later be convicted of anarchy, which was a misdemeanor in Arkansas. He would be fined $500 and sent to work in California by the Socialist Party. This event occurred in the early days of the union when Mitchell and the leadership were still radical. But the crowd's reaction is instructive[23] for how the rank and file must have felt. Were Rodgers and Mitchell seen as the new liberating army? We will never know for sure, but the crowd's reaction reveals the relief they felt when someone with power said what they had said for years in the privacy of their homes.

As union members and leaders armed themselves for self-defense the violence continued. In May 1937 W. B. Moore of Blythville, Arkansas, wrote to J. R. Butler to report that county officials were attempting to scare members out of the union by displaying "their guns and black jacks." He reported that many of his members were scared and some were leaving town.[24] This violence continued until the union was finally forced to stop organizing in 1938. By then the union was a shell of itself, having been defeated by violence, coercion, and intimidation. Faced with violent suppression, men and women packed up their meager belongings and left the cotton lands.

As part of the "reign of terror" that followed the 1935 and 1936 strikes, many landowners began an organized effort to remove any STFU member from their land.[25] The union received daily letters from sharecropper and tenant farmer families revealing how widespread the evictions were.

Landlords proved that they were willing to use any means necessary to discipline their workforce, including murder. This viscous backlash taught union leaders that they could not fight landowners without some power behind them. But more importantly, it taught rank and file sharecroppers and tenant farmers that they were not safe as union members.

Mechanization exacerbated the union's situation. Southern farmers had little money to invest in machines to increase their production. Before the 1930s, a number of factors retarded cotton mechanization. The most important was the large supply of cheap labor available to prepare land, plant seed, hoe weeds, and pick cotton. In addition, tractors were very expensive. Most farmers lacked capital to buy them, and most banks were wary of extending credit. The early machines also did not have the ability to weed and pick cotton. A study of three Arkansas delta counties from 1932 to 1938 discovered that tractors were most commonly used for plowing, disking, and cutting cotton stalks. Tractors, in other words, were used simply for seedbed preparation, not for the labor-intensive picking.[26] The landlord still had to retain a labor force to plant, hoe, and pick cotton.[27] It would be after World War II before southern farms introduced the cotton picker.

Before World War I the United States Department of Agriculture, agricultural colleges, agricultural experiment stations, and farm magazine editors had encouraged tractor use to increase efficiency and profitability.[28] The farmers' aversion to tractors had slowly begun to abate during World War I when International Harvester's promotional efforts had introduced many farmers to the new farm machines. Mechanization had begun in the western United States and over the years slowly moved across the South. When the New Deal arrived and interjected AAA money, many farmers began to invest in tractors because of this earlier propaganda.[29]

Therefore, the New Deal's plan to provide money to landowners through the Agriculture Adjustment Administration (AAA) came as a great boost. For the first time, many farmers had the money they needed to invest in machinery. Use of tractors grew at an astounding rate in the 1930s. Between 1930 and 1940 the number of tractors in Arkansas counties that had STFU locals grew by 182.63 percent. In 1937 alone, southern landowners bought more tractors than had been enumerated on the 1920 census.[30]

Historian Gilbert Fite has suggested that mechanization meant "much more than simply buying a two-row or four-row equipment." It meant "recognizing farm operations and changing relationships between land and people."[31] The most important social transformation that occurred with the coming of the tractor was the displacement of large numbers of tenants and the increase of day laborers. C. Horace Hamilton reported that "the displacement of three to five families by one tractor [was] not uncommon."[32]

The tractor pushed sharecroppers and tenant farmers out of their traditional jobs and many of them became day laborers. Mitchell explained to the Committee on Interstate Migration in 1940 that because of mechanization the union's membership had changed through the years. "In 1934, ninety percent of the members . . . were either tenant farmers or sharecroppers, but by 1937 sixty percent of the members became day laborers and today [1940] over seventy-five percent are working for wages."[33] Without the sharecroppers and tenant farmers, it became much harder for the STFU to find men and women to organize.

Despite the impact of both violence and mechanization, the union's demise cannot be attributed solely to external forces. The union also faced serious internal problems. In the past, historians have noted that the union had internal difficulties, but have focused on the conflict between socialist and communist leaders that culminated in the discovery that Claude Williams, one of the union's most trusted leaders, was working to place the STFU under Communist Party control. Although that conflict is important, there is no evidence that the majority of the union's rank and file was ever concerned with this dispute. Discussion of the STFU's internal conflicts needs to be shifted from factions and fighting among leaders to the conflict that existed between the rank and file's aspirations and the leaders' goals and agendas. The issue is not an argument between an unerring rank and file and a deceptive leadership. The leaders of the STFU, both socialist and communist, were firmly committed to rank and file goals most of the time. Union leaders wanted these men and women to get ahead and have economic security. But the leaders' political philosophy and the rank and file's needs came into serious conflict.

Race issues plagued the union from its earliest days. While the first local may have been consciously integrated, other locals were segregated; leaders were assigned tasks by race; and many African-Americans left the union because they believed the white leaders were not looking out for their best interests.

Some historians have praised the STFU's claim to be integrated. Historian Jerold S. Auerbach called the STFU "militantly class conscious and avowedly interracial, it ran roughshod over local prejudices."[34] Donald H. Grubbs, the author of the most significant work on the STFU, even argues that "within the STFU America's greatest problem, that of race relations, was solved as well as any realistic observer could expect."[35]

While there is no doubt that men like H. L. Mitchell and Howard Kester were more racially sensitive then most of their contemporaries, it does seem that these men were still limited by the segregationist rhetoric and practice of their time. They were not a racially sensitive vanguard that so many historians have made them out to be.

Black and white people had separate places in the South. This was also true within the STFU. While there were some integrated locals, it seems that it was much more common to have segregated locals. Leon Turner, an African-American sharecropper from Altheimer, Arkansas, was saddened that white members wanted to set up a segregated local.[36] White members often wrote asking for information about segregated locals. J. P. Martain of Sheridan, Arkansas, wanted an all-white local in Sheridan, but Mitchell was forced to tell him that there were only "Negro locals" in that county.[37] After a short time this segregation became a part of the union's culture. In a 1936 form for local secretaries to fill out a standard line asked if locals were "white or colored."[38]

Beyond segregated locals the STFU also had separate organizers and leaders for each race. It was usually assumed that white organizers should organize whites, and black organizers blacks. Locals would write to the

Union headquarters asking for a certain organizer, and leaders assumed that since the races were separate in the South the union should work within that system. In reality this was probably the only way the union could have stayed in existence. Had organizers actually tried to live out the rhetoric of racial equality they might, as they feared, have started another Elaine. This is a long cry from challenging the southern race system that so many historians claim for the STFU.[39]

In an attempt to live up to their rhetoric of racial equality the Union's white leaders established a policy at the national level—the union's president would be white and the vice-president would be black. This solution satisfied H. L. Mitchell, Howard Kester, and Norman Thomas, but as African-American's membership grew its dissatisfaction with racial relations within the union also caused them to become more vocal.

This African-American dissatisfaction arose from many sources. E. B. McKinney, a 64-year-old National Baptist preacher, tended to be the dominant spokesperson for African-American issues on the STFU's Executive Council. In 1936 he was concerned with food and clothing for "his people." He and Mitchell had real ideological differences on this issue, but it would take a racial tone. Mitchell firmly believed that giving members food or clothing from the national office would be "disastrous" to an organization that was supposed to fight for people's rights. McKinney believed it was simple Christian charity for the STFU to use its money for the poor. Tactically McKinney believed it would convince black members that white leaders understood their plight. As an example, and to chide Mitchell for ignoring this group, McKinney explained that the all black locals of Jefferson County, Arkansas, were in great need of help, but it seemed no matter how many times they wrote to Memphis, Mitchell ignored them. Why should they struggle for the union if the union would not struggle for them?[40]

Beyond the issue of ignoring black locals, many black organizers felt their needs were being ignored. Organizers like McKinney and John Handcox, a black sharecropper and songwriter for the union, did not understand why they were being asked to sacrifice so much while Mitchell and other white leaders sat in relative safety in Memphis. McKinney and Handcox wanted better pay, and they wanted their families to be safe. Mitchell and McKinney's relationship soured even more in April 1936 when Mitchell emphatically told McKinney, "I am afraid the union can not support your family." McKinney and other black members were beginning to doubt the union's commitment to them.[41]

Through the late spring and summer of 1936 the union was rocked by race concerns. McKinney and other black leaders wrote to white leaders laying out their grievances and offering practical solutions. The issue was the union's practice of sending rank and file members to labor schools to learn how to be organizers. Up to this time the union had only sent white members. McKinney and Reverend A. B. Brookins wanted to know why black men were not being sent. After explaining their complaint, they recommended that from this point on the union send one black member and one white member to any school or meeting.[42]

Mitchell's response to these complaints was telling. To McKinney and Brookins he simply explained that the union did not discriminate; it was simply looking for "competent" people, regardless of race. They told McKinney it was time for him to put aside his concern for race. Instead, he should concern himself with the important issues of class. "The solidarity of black and white workers is much more important than what happens to a white or black man. Who cares if it has happened before and it will happen again." "Who cares," these words must have resonated in McKinney's brain. For a white man to say injustice had happened and would surely happen again is one thing, but for a black man or woman who lived that injustice on a day to day basis it must have been a sorrowful thing to hear.[43]

In early 1937 McKinney would begin his long torturous road out of the union. In January McKinney resigned from the union. He was finally tired of being put off by the white leaders. When asked to explain, McKinney simply wrote, "the matters which refer to the Negro is the last to be considered." J. R. Butler, the white union president, once again chided McKinney for race thinking and asked him to please think along class lines. After much haggling McKinney stayed with the STFU as a "representative of my group."[44]

In the fall of 1937 racial issues would come to a head. By this time the STFU had joined the Congress of Industrial Organizations (CIO) as a part of the United Cannery, Agricultural, Packing, and Allied Workers of America (UCAPAWA) headed by communist member Donald Henderson. At the STFU convention in 1937 Claude Williams, a white preacher, schoolteacher, and friend of Donald Henderson, attempted to wrestle control of the STFU from H. L. Mitchell and Howard Kester.

Williams had arrived at the convention ten days early attempting to persuade African American members to vote for his resolutions. The first action he introduced on the convention floor was a statement committing the STFU to opposing both racial discrimination and racial segregation. Mitchell was horrified. He believed that this resolution would "commit southern white men to social equality." Mitchell believed this would destroy the union. When the resolution passed, Mitchell announced to friends of the Union, "the Southern Tenant Farmers' union in reality is no longer an organization following the convention which adjourned here today."[45]

After this resolution was passed, Claude Williams attempted to have an all-black executive committee elected. In place of Mitchell, who was nominated by the old executive board to continue his job, Williams nominated a young African-American sharecropper named Leon Turner. When it appeared that Turner would win, Howard Kester took to the floor and appealed for delegates to elect the man who was most qualified. In the end Mitchell's job was saved when the convention amended the constitution to allow for two secretaries.[46]

Throughout the convention Mitchell seemed to miss the animosity that the black members felt towards the white leaders. At the end of the convention, Mitchell blamed the racial strife solely on Williams and his agitation for Donald Henderson. In Mitchell's words, "a feeling of prejudice . . . had not existed in our organization before."[47]

African Americans would continue to feel dissatisfied with the Mitchell-controlled STFU. Although few historians know about it, there was an anti-Mitchell STFU founded by black members in 1940. One newspaper from their organization still exists. This union stayed with the CIO when Mitchell's group left.[48] In the end this racial strife that came to a head at the 1937 convention would cause many members to leave the union.

For his part Mitchell was glad to report to Clay East in 1939 that they had left the CIO and there was a new vice-president, F. R. Betton, "a straight forward fellow with good education, a justice of peace in his township, surveyor of cotton lands for the AAA, etc. despite the fact that he is black as the ace of spades."[49] Obviously Mitchell was still a man trapped in his time, not as he liked to claim, a part of the racial vanguard.

The union's racial divisions might have been strong enough to wound the union, but it also suffered from one other internal problem. From the union's earliest days rank and file members made clear what their aspirations and goals were. Sharecroppers and tenant farmers were concerned primarily about short-term problems such as food, clothing, and a place to live. When they wrote for help, sharecroppers and tenant farmers usually received letters that reveal STFU leaders as compassionate people. J. R. Butler's reply to Henderson Bentley's 1937 letter is an example. The very day that he received the letter Butler responded: "I would like to help you. I would like to help every poor person in the world but I can't. I am poor too. The Union can not help for as I told you we do not have the money to help with."[50]

As it became painfully obvious that New Deal agricultural policy was not going to help the majority of sharecroppers and tenant farmers, union leaders began to call for cooperative farming to replace the sharecropping and tenant system. This decision placed the leadership in opposition to the long-term wishes for land ownership that the rank and file clearly articulated. This was a major reason why men and women left the STFU in droves.

The leaders' call for cooperative farming had a long history in American radicalism. The majority of union leaders were Socialist Party members. In the late nineteenth century, with the dramatic growth of the northern factory system and the growing tension between farmers, railroads, and banks, workers and farmers launched open revolts in the South and West against the factory system and the power held by railroads and banks. Workers and farmers had many strategic options to choose from: Greenbackism, the single tax plan, cooperatives, the Farmers Alliance, and socialism. Each of these options originated in an earlier republican ideology that held that all men should be independent, hard-working, and virtuous. Workers and farmers had used this republicanism to analyze changes in the economic system and to offer alternatives to capitalism.[51]

There were two distinct strains of American socialism, one primarily immigrant and the other native. Immigrant socialists struggled to appeal to the native born American public in an American political idiom, but for the most part, they failed. In 1874, for example, the Workingman's Party of Illinois and the Social-Democratic Workingmen's Party of North America were defeated in state elections when the Party presented a ticket completely dominated by German-speaking candidates.[52] Immigrant socialists tended to use the language of European radicalism rather than that of the American republican tradition.

Socialism also developed a native strain. Initially non-Marxist, this native socialism grew out of the diverse ways Americans had dealt with economic change. Eventually some of these socialists would become Marxists, but others traced their radical origins back to Thomas Paine, Thomas Jefferson, spiritualism, and the New Testament. Oscar Ameringer is a case in point. Ameringer was born in Germany, but had immigrated to the United States at an early age and spent his formative years of intellectual development in his new country. Ameringer later stated that he discovered industrial unionism, Jeffersonian democracy, and Mark Twain's humor before he studied Marx. These ideas, according to James Green, contributed to his development as a socialist. Marxist ideas came after his radicalism was established.[53]

Radical groups, from the Farmer's Alliance to socialists, had to develop a position on the "land question." Socialists' plans for restructuring agriculture were essential tools for gaining votes in local and national elections. In 1912 alone, four southwestern agricultural states—Oklahoma, Louisiana, Texas, and Arkansas—gave Eugene Debs one-tenth of his national vote for the presidency.[54] If the Socialists were going to win elections, they realized, they would have to win more agricultural states.

The American Socialist Party decided at the turn of the century that it could not continue to hold to Marx's idea that farmers were simply capitalists; instead, they theorized that farmers were workers whose interests could best be met by the Socialist Party's platform.[55] The 1912 party platform reflected this principle when it stated that the Socialist Party would encourage the development of farming cooperatives.[56] This idea of cooperatives persisted for the next twenty-five years and was still the Socialist Party position in 1934. Norman Thomas, who would greatly influence H. L. Mitchell and other STFU leaders, believed that farming cooperatives would save the American South.[57]

STFU national leaders, mostly members of the Socialist and Communist parties, fully accepted cooperative farming principles. But union leaders were overwhelmed by the amount of work they faced when they entered the Arkansas delta in 1934. An examination of documents they produced in 1934 and 1935 shows that there were very few references to "land for the landless" or to "cooperative farming," terms commonly used in Socialist Party platforms. Mitchell had spent the summer and fall of 1934 traveling around Arkansas cotton-growing counties attempting to learn all he could about sharecropper and tenant farmers' demands. What he saw overwhelmed him. Their living conditions were abysmal; they ate poorly; and they had no rights except those given to them by their bosses. If they tried to appeal to outside forces such as police or courts they were laughed at and told to go back to work or they would be sent to the penitentiary. Many Poinsett County sharecroppers and tenant farmers knew that Mitchell could be trusted, and they quickly laid out for him what they wanted.

The things Mitchell saw on his 1934 trip through cotton country, and the ideas found in the deluge of letters from sharecroppers and tenant farmers that were streaming into his Tyronza, Arkansas, business, were reflected in the first STFU program found in the membership book. This booklet was given to each sharecropper and tenant farmer when he or she joined the union. Mitchell was concerned that potential members know in simple terms what the union's "sole purpose" was. The union was not concerned with cooperative farming at this point, only in "securing better living conditions through decent contracts and higher wages for farm labor."[58] This would have sounded like a standard union contract for any industrial group had he not placed the words "farm labor" at the end. There was no promise of cooperatives, just hope for a better life.

Not only did the union's early program reflect the views of the rank and file, but the Union in 1934 was also actively attempting to support sharecroppers and tenant farmers who were evicted or not given their share of Agricultural Adjustment Act parity money. In November 1934 the union set up a Legal Defense Fund to support "all members of the union who [were] threatened with eviction from the land."[59]

The STFU was growing rapidly by 1935. By the winter of that year the union had established an eleven-point program:

1. All farm labor, sharecroppers, renters, etc. be given representation on all boards of control designed to aid agriculture.
2. Enforcement of all government contracts, specifically section 7 of the AAA plan with payments being made directly to the Sharecroppers and Tenant Farmers.
3. Eviction from the land to be stopped.
4. Free schools and busses to transport our children to school (and textbooks)
5. Right to unionize with protection.
6. Decent wages, hours and conditions for all farm labor.
7. Adequate cash furnished during the farming season at a legal rate of interest, with privilege of trading were we want.
8. Pay at prevailing wages for all improvements on property of owners.
9. Decent houses for each family, with right to use part of the land for free for growing food-stuff.
10. Access to woodland owned by landlord, to secure fuel wood for personal use.
11. Right to sell cotton at market price and to whom we please.

These demands reflect most of the immediate goals that sharecroppers and tenant farmers made to union leaders in 1934 and 1935. It is important to note that they did not demand land redistribution so they could work it collectively. The reforms they demanded would have kept the sharecropping system in place; they simply would have given sharecroppers and tenant farmers greater control over their lives. Nevertheless, STFU leadership was already beginning to move away from this practical but limited program. In 1935 the Union produced its first constitution in which the term "cooperative society" is found. After stating that the union's aim was to "protect our rights and interests as individuals by collective action," it announced that the STFU wished to "establish a co-operative society." Mitchell did not explain what he meant by this term, but he hinted at his future position when he said, "The earth is the common heritage of all, we maintain that the use and occupancy of the land should be the sole title."[60]

In 1935 J. R. Butler made the STFU's first contact with a government agency to articulate the union's position on the cotton South's situation. Butler wrote to Colonel Lawrence Westbrook, who had recently become the Rehabilitation Administration's head. This federal agency was responsible for lending individual families money so they could purchase tools, seed, and livestock. Historian Donald Holley has described the program's objective as taking farm families off relief rolls and placing them back on farms full-time.[61] Butler wanted Westbrook to know that there was a southern organization that was interested in what happened to the growing number of evicted sharecroppers and tenant farmers. He also wanted Westbrook to know that the STFU would support any plan devised to aid dispossessed farmers. Then he advanced his own plan that called for people who owned a home to be given a track of land sufficient for them and their family to live comfortably. The government would guarantee that "as long as they occupy and use the land they will be protected in its possession" and the government would hold the title to the land "forever."[62] In his letter Butler offered plan two of the proposals discussed earlier: sharecroppers and tenant farmers would have become renters, a higher stage of tenant farming that guaranteed a certain amount of autonomy. It is significant that landowners were to be expelled from the land and that the new landlord was to be the government. Throughout the letters of sharecroppers and tenant farmers there is a recurring theme that the government would make a better landowner than the individuals who then controlled the land. This was a step away from sharecropping toward individuals working their own land for profit.

None of the 1934 and 1935 plans embodied the cooperative plans that would become part of future STFU programs. These early programs grew out of observations by leaders of the sharecroppers and tenant farmers' immediate needs and the persistent demands that sharecroppers and tenant farmers actually made. These early programs and the 1935 strike attempted to humanize the sharecropping and tenant farming system without overthrowing it. But the needs of sharecroppers and tenant farmers were changing rapidly. With more and more farmers being thrown off the land, the attempt to humanize sharecropping was becoming more untenable with each passing month.

For the first half of 1936, union leaders continued in the same manner as they had in 1934 and 1935. They were planning another strike for September. But by November 1936 conditions had changed. Howard Kester became the pivotal STFU leader and radically redirected its position on the land question.

In the early summer of 1936 after the cotton crop had been "laid by," union leaders again stated that their only aim was to "improve the living conditions of the farmers in the South."[63] During the summer, union leaders had decided that it was time for another strike. Again, they planned to strike when the cotton was ready for picking, hoping that planters would have to negotiate with sharecroppers and tenant farmers as they had in 1935. In a letter written in May 1936, Mitchell listed strike demands:

> 1. A unified contract guaranteeing legal rates of interest on furnishings, payment in full of government subsidies, parity, etc., wage rates not less than $1.00 per 10 hour day, 15 cents per hour for overtime day labor.
> 2. Right to form a union and not to be discriminated on account of union membership.[64]

The 1936 strike failed miserably. Word of the work stoppage leaked to landlords, who were ready and willing to use the vicious intimidation tactics of the previous year to keep their laborers in the fields.[65] With the 1936 strike defeat, mass evictions intensified. Facing a profound crisis, union leaders were desperate for fresh help and new ideas.

This infusion came from Howard Kester, a fiery young Christian socialist. Kester was born in Martinsville, Virginia in 1904. As a young man he decided that he wanted to become a minister and began to pursue his "calling." Kester believed that the application of modern science and Christian faith to social problems could establish the Kingdom of God on earth.[66] In 1936 Kester was chosen by Southern Tenant Farmers' Union leaders to represent them before the Arkansas Governor's Commission on Farm Tenancy. There Kester presented a passionate and sometimes vivid description of the horrendous living conditions of sharecroppers and tenant farmers and was also able to describe the civil rights violations against STFU members. At the end of his presentation, Kester began his analysis of the cotton South's situation. His main fear was the coming of the cotton-picking machine. He saw that this new machine, first tested by the socialist Rust brothers, meant "the expulsion from the land of hundreds of thousands of men whose jobs will be performed by the machine." In a recent test, he reported, the machine had picked in one day the amount formerly picked by forty people.[67] Kester also reported that the most recent census data revealed that southern tenancy was declining. These tenants, Kester argued, were not moving up to independent farm ownership but were being forced down to the status of day laborers.[68] The landlord had no legal or customary obligations to day laborers, as he did to sharecroppers and tenant farmers. Day laborers worked for 35 to 75 cents a day and had to find a place to live and a way to feed their families. Kester demanded to know, "What will become of the millions of men, women, and children" who were losing all they had ever known?[69] Kester offered a nine-point plan that he believed would lead to "a more wholesome life in Arkansas."

1. Education must be increased. Education for children and adults and for blacks and whites.
2. Protection of all civil rights.
3. Right of labor to organize.
4. Strengthen the State Department of Labor.
5. Protection against misuse of the lien system and give croppers the right to sue if they feel they are being used.
6. Abolish the plantation commissary and allow tenants to trade wherever they chose.
7. Enforce the legal rate of interest.
8. Abolish the poll tax.
9. Co-operative farming.

This plan generally sounded like the 1934 and 1935 programs that union leaders had offered. The desire to meet union members' immediate needs was still the union leadership's central goal. The radical difference was point nine in which the union leaders added cooperative farming to the list. Rank and file members had rejected this way of farming in 1935 and had continued to write letters stating that they wanted autonomy and their own land to farm. Clearly, Kester had taken a first step away from rank and file conceptions of the STFU's purpose.

In 1936 Kester also wrote a book entitled, *Revolt Among the Sharecroppers* in which he told the story of the STFU's struggles to a large national audience. In the last few pages, he discussed what he believed it would take to heal the cotton South. He called tenancy a "cancerous growth" and argued that "nothing short of a major operation will suffice to rid us of its evils."[70] The operation he had in mind was the ending of absentee landlordism and the tenancy system. He based this argument upon the idea seen in embryo earlier that the land should belong to those who occupy and use it.[71] Kester suggested that the government establish farms for those who would use land and not for those who would simply speculate on it. A Federal Land Authority would govern this new land redistribution scheme.[72] Kester made it clear that the Land Authority would not establish small independent farms. He believed that in a changing economic world in which mechanization and expanding world competition were raising farming costs, small farms would lead to the creation of a "peasant class of farmers."[73] Instead, Kester argued that only on cooperative farms could people bring together the resources needed to engage in large-scale modern farming.[74]

Kester was again arguing for cooperative farming in the waning days of 1936. In a speech, "The Human Side of Cotton Tenancy," he argued that "tenancy is itself an evil . . . that must be abolished." He argued that a new type of communal farming needed to be developed. He provided a list of economic and moral advantages that cooperative farming would have over the existing tenant system as well as over small-scale individually owned farms.[75]

For Kester cooperative farming made good economic sense. It allowed economic and agricultural experts to plan crop rotations and to control soil erosion. Cooperative farming also allowed for the use of tractors that individual small farmers could not afford. It allowed workers to buy food, clothes, and farming supplies in bulk, which lowered the individual's cost and raised the quality of goods. One danger of small farming, Kester believed, was that in hard times the farmer only had his good name for support, a collateral that lenders were not willing to accept given nature's capriciousness and farming's uncertainty. Kester believed that if operated well, cooperative farms would have a better chance of surviving economic hard times.

Far more important than these economic arguments to Kester were moral arguments favoring cooperative farming. The cooperative farming system would allow people to use their natural skills in different areas of the farm through the division of labor. Cooperative farms would also bring people closer in communal villages. Under the existing system of tenancy, sharecroppers and tenant farmers were spread out over a large land area; the cooperative system that Kester envisioned had people living together in groups of one hundred or less. Most important of all for Kester, the cooperative vision would begin to undo the individualist myth that had enveloped farming in America. "A group spirit of accomplishment would replace individual pride," he wrote.[76]

As 1936 ended, union leaders had come a long way from their original program of immediate humanization of sharecropping and tenant farming. The STFU program still reflected these short-term demands, but whenever union leaders appeared before government commissions or petitioned government agencies they increasingly stressed cooperative farming, not the rank and file's immediate needs or their vision of autonomous landownership.

Why would union leaders move away from the wishes and desires that sharecroppers and tenant farmers had made so clear? There are at least three reasons the STFU leadership began to promote cooperative thinking. Union leaders were finally focusing on their socialist ideology. By late 1936 and 1937 Howard Kester and Claude Williams' Christian socialism came to dominate the STFU leadership. In Christian socialism all men and women were seen to be brothers and sisters because they shared a common creation. Although relations between Kester and Williams would rupture over allegations that Williams was a communist trying to take control of the STFU, both believed that all men and women, black and white, were created in God's image and that the Earth was created for all people to use equally. Flowing from these theological presuppositions both men encouraged union leaders to continually petition the government for a more just form of farming, which to Kester and Williams meant the cooperative method.[77]

The second reason union leaders moved away from the membership's views on land was the 1935 relocation of union headquarters from Tyronza, Arkansas, to Memphis, Tennessee. In one sense, this move was necessary and helpful. Mitchell and other union leaders were under constant death threats while they lived in Arkansas. By moving to Memphis, they faded into the tapestry of people that flowed daily in and out of the city. On the other hand, this move put the leaders out of daily contact with sharecroppers and tenant farmers who previously had come by the Tyronza, Arkansas, office to share their views and concerns. With this loss of daily contact union leaders lost the daily reminder that they represented a nonsocialist rank and file.

The last reason that caused leaders to articulate views that did not represent those of sharecroppers and tenant farmers was their reaction to the Bankhead bill that had been introduced in the United States Senate by Alabama Senator John H. Bankhead. This bill, which was still being debated in 1936, would have established the Farm Security Administration to provide low-interest loans to landless farmers to allow them to buy their own farms.[78] To STFU leaders, this bill contradicted the principles of cooperative farming to which they were so strongly committed. In reaction to the individualist assumptions of the Bankhead bill, STFU leaders believed that "Through co-operative farming a new altogether, type of rural life may be developed in the South. By drawing groups of farmers together into a co-operative community they may have at their disposal all of the resources of modern civilization."[79] For these three reasons, 1936 was the pivotal year when union leaders moved away from the desires of their rank and file.

Despite this growing split, union leaders were not deaf to the cry from the cotton fields. Each was a compassionate person who simply failed to understand the sharecropper and tenant farmers' desire for land.[80] Of all the leaders H. L. Mitchell was the one who tried hardest to reconcile the leadership position with that of the rank and file. In early January 1937 Mitchell spoke in Dallas, Texas, before the President's Special Committee on Farm Tenancy. Mitchell's speech was a long and passionate appeal to his listeners' hearts. He described sharecropper and tenant farmers' wretched living and working conditions. He also laid out Union leaders' solutions for the tenant-farming problem. Unlike the program written by Kester, Mitchell's plan called for two forms of farming—cooperative and individual. But even

Mitchell did not perceive these farms as equal. He stressed cooperative over individual farming. The union leadership called on the government to educate people in the efficiency of collective farming.[81]

In March 1937 Mitchell helped the Oklahoma Southern Tenant Farmers' Union formulate its legislative program. In it, union leaders stated that "the great mass of people can no longer succeed by individual effort." The program again called for both forms of farming but with major stress on cooperative farming. This proposal demonstrated how Mitchell reconciled two conflicting philosophies: large cotton-growing areas would be made up of cooperative farming groups and small isolated tracts of good highland farmland would be utilized for individual farming.[82] With this program, union leaders tried to communicate their vision for the cotton-growing South and placate sharecroppers and tenant farmers who wanted to own their own land.

Although STFU leaders never stopped including immediate needs in the proposals they made to government commissions and agencies, sharecroppers and tenant farmers knew that they still lacked food, decent clothing, and a house to live in. Sharecroppers and tenant farmers also still believed that they were being singled out for eviction because of their Union membership. It was obvious to many sharecroppers and tenant farmers by 1937 that the union could not or would not help them with these immediate needs. The rank and file also found that their long-term goal of land ownership would not be met. Feeling betrayed because union leaders seemed to be spending all their time and money fighting for cooperatives, a method of farming that sharecroppers and tenant farmers had already rejected, many rank and file members became frustrated with the union and left.

This growing frustration among members erupted at the 1938 STFU convention when delegate J. E. Clayton rose to complain, "I don't think the national office is paying enough attention to some of the complaints about relief grants." J. R. Butler, president of the union, rose, obviously confused by this attack, and offered a rambling reply that the leadership had worked night and day to help sharecroppers and tenant farmers. Clayton obviously was not convinced and left the Union.[83] Henderson Bently and J. E. Clayton were among the many sharecroppers and tenant farmers who moved into the limelight of history and then as quickly disappeared into its shadows. Their stories were recounted in the union's history, the testimonies of people who had placed all their hopes and dreams in the Union and in the end were left feeling betrayed and alone.

Mitchell would later claim that the last show of the Union's strength was a rally on July 4, 1938, in Parkin, Arkansas.[84] The Southern Tenant Farmers' Union was a mere skeleton by 1940. Few sharecroppers and tenant farmers still placed trust in the organization. Although the union would continue to organize in the Arkansas delta until 1945, it had essentially died by 1940.

The STFU was born in a time of great change. The union came into the Arkansas delta believing that it could win. But by January 1936, a violent backlash had begun. Coupled with the introduction of tractors that displaced sharecroppers and tenant farmers, violence probably would have destroyed the union anyway. To make matters worse, the union also faced formidable internal crises.

Sharecroppers, tenant farmers, and union leaders ultimately held two different visions of how society should be organized. Sharecroppers and tenant farmers wanted their immediate needs met, and they wanted land to call their own. STFU leaders, on the other hand, shifted their vision throughout the years. In the early days of the STFU, they attempted to articulate the rank and file's demands and visions. But over time their position began to change. Union leaders began to demand a way of farming that sharecroppers and tenant farmers had rejected. In the end, this shift in STFU policy and the union's inability to provide for the basic needs of its rank and file would be important causes for the union's demise. In addition rank and file members maintained a fundamentalist religious vision of the world quite at odds with the secularist or social gospel vision of their leaders.

The STFU came to a swift end. H. L. Mitchell shocked the seventh annual STFU convention in 1941 when he announced that he saw "no basis for trade unionism in southern agriculture."[85] In that one sentence Mitchell admitted defeat. Although the union would limp along for four more years, it really lived on only in name. In 1945, the union closed its office in Memphis for good, quietly leaving the Arkansas delta.

EPILOGUE

SHARECROPPERS AND TENANT FARMERS must be returned to the forefront of Southern Tenant Farmers' Union story. These men and women mattered in history, and it is a tragedy there their story is now all but forgotten. These men and women, both black and white, believed that they could appeal to the government and to the land owners to see that their Christian duty lay in helping the poor in their midst. To this effect they created the STFU to act as their collective voice. These men and women joined the STFU looking for a way to provide a better and richer life for their families. Instead they found themselves thrown out of the world most of them had known their whole lives. They drew upon Christianity to analyze the world around them and to provide a solution to their problems. Their world was a moral world in which men and women were judged on the basis of how they loved God and helped their neighbor. Within the union they took care of one another and with the union they attempted to change the personal agendas of New Deal leaders according to their own vision of a decent and just society. They failed to gain either their short-term or long-term goals. Although they failed in their agenda, they remained faithful to their view of the world, and to them this was of extreme importance.

One union historian believed that if you stopped your car out on the edge of Highway 63 near Marked Tree, you could hear voices singing in the distance—"The union is a-marching, we shall not be Moved. . . ."[1] By this he wanted his readers to close his book with the understanding that this was a defiant union, that although it was beaten, the reader could learn a lesson about organizing people to fight for justice. I have no argument with this, but as I stand out on that same stretch of highway I also hear another song flowing in over the dark and deserted cotton fields, "Well I was farming shares and always I was poor. My debts they were so many they wouldn't go around. Drought got my crop and Mr. Banker took my home.—I ain't got no home in this world any more."[2]

Many of the sharecroppers and tenant farmers who lost their farms would eventually find jobs in the war industries that would develop with United States entry into World War II. Many left the rural worlds they had known forever and eventually learned to live in new environments, while some even prospered in California and Chicago. Many others did prosper and many of these men and women still sit in the delta, with their children and grandchildren. Many have been able to get a small house, some even to buy a tiny piece of land. But most simply made it from day to day.

In the town of Birdsong, Arkansas I came across a group of men and women looking out over the fields they and their fathers had once hoped to own. A large mechanical cotton picker did the work in one day that it would have taken a family a week to do in the 1930s. No one really grieves the loss of the sharecropping system. The despair one finds in some in the delta is the despair of dreams betrayed and of hopes crushed. These men and women that hot August day in 1991 sat in a circle of chairs under a large oak at the edge of an old cotton field and told stories. They laughed at the old times, they raged at their losses, and cried for the injustices they had endured. In the end they passed the bottle around the circle one more time and with a silent sorrow they realized they had failed to possess the land.

NOTES

INTRODUCTION

1. Frederick Buechner, *The Alphabet of Grace* (San Francisco: Harper San Francisco, 1970), 3–4.

2. Arkansas Democrat Gazette, "Union for Farmworkers Marks 75th Anniversary." By Nancy Cole, http://www.nwanews.com/adg/national/264151/, Accessed 20 July 2009.

3. H. L. Mitchell, *Mean Things Happening in This Land: The Life and Times of H. L. Mitchell Co-founder of the Southern Tenant Farmer's Union* (Monticlair, N. J.: Allanheld, Osmun, 1979).

4. Although Mitchell did not publish his book until the late 1970s, he was sought out and used as a source for information by every historian who wrote on the STFU.

5. Mark Naison, "The Southern Tenant Farmers' Union and the CIO," Radical/America 2, (1968) 36.

6. M. S. Venkataramani, "Norman Thomas, Arkansas Sharecroppers, and the Roosevelt Agricultural Policies, 1933–1937," *Mississippi Valley Historical Review* 47 (September 1960); Jerold Auerbach, "Southern Tenant Farmers: Socialist Critics of the New Deal," *Labor History* 7 (Winter 1966); Donald H. Grubbs, *A Cry From The Cotton* (Chapel Hill: University of North Carolina Press, 1971).

7. Pete Daniel, *Standing at the Crossroads: Southern Life in the Twentieth Century*. (New York: Hill and Wang, 1986), 121–122.

8. Lawrence Goodwyn, *Democratic Promise: The Populist Movement in America* (New York: Oxford University Press).

9. Donald H. Grubbs, *Cry From The Cotton*, 66–68.

10. Herbert G. Gutman and Donald H. Bell, ed., *The New England Working Class and the New Labor History* (Urbana: University of Illinois Press, 1987), xiv.

CHAPTER ONE

1. George P. Rawick, *The American Slave: A Composite Autobiography Series Two, Volume Seven* (Westport: Greenwood Press, Inc., 1972), 85–87.

2. Interview with Ida Davis by Jim Ross, Tape recorded January 4, 1984 and February 7, 1985.

3. Shlomowitz, Ralph. "The Origins of Southern Sharecropping," *Agricultural History*, 53 (July 1979): 557–75.

4. For the evolution of the tenancy system see: Ira Berlin, et al., "The Wartime Genesis of Free Labor, 1861–1865" in *Slaves No More: Three Essays in Emancipation and the Civil War* (Cambridge: Cambridge University Press, 1990), 79–186; Ronald L. F. Davis, *Good and Faithful Labor: From Slavery to Sharecropping in the Natchez District, 1860–1890* (Westport: Greenwood Press, Inc., 1982); Barbara Jeanne Fields, *Slavery and Freedom on the Middle Ground: Maryland during the Nineteenth Century* (New Haven: Yale University Press, 1985), 131–206; Eric Foner, *Nothing But Freedom: Emancipation and Its Legacy* (Baton Rouge: Louisiana State University Press, 1983); Eric Foner, *Reconstruction: America's Unfinished Revolution, 1863–1877* (New York: Harper & Row, Pub., 1988); Thavolia Glymph, et. al., *Essays on the Postbellum Southern Economy* (College Station: Texas A&M University Press, 1985); Robert Higgs, *Cooperation and Coercion: Blacks in the American Economy, 1865–1914* (Cambridge: Cambridge University Press, 1977); Jay R. Mandle, *Not Slave, Not Free: The African American Economic Experience Since the Civil War* (Durham: Duke University Press, 1992); Donald Nieman, ed., *From Slavery to Sharecropping: White Land and Black Labor in the Rural South, 1865–1900* (New York: Garland Press, 1994); Roger L. Ransom and Richard Sutch, *One Kind of Freedom: The Economic Consequences of Emancipation* (Cambridge: Cambridge University Press, 1977); Joseph P. Reidy, *From Slavery to Agrarian Capitalism in the Cotton Plantation South: Central Georgia, 1800–1880* (Chapel Hill: The University of North Carolina Press, 1992); Julie Saville, *The Work of Reconstruction: From Slave to Wage Labor in South Carolina, 1860–1870* (Cambridge: Cambridge University Press, 1994); Vernon Lane Wharton, *The Negro in Mississippi, 1865–1890* (New York: Harper & Row, Publishers, 1965); Jeannie M. Whayne, Ed., *Shadows Over Sunnyside: An Arkansas Plantation in Transition, 1830–1845* (Fayetteville: University of Arkansas Press, 1993); Jonathan M. Wiener, *Social Origins of the New South: Alabama, 1860–1885* (Baton Rouge: Louisiana State University Press, 1978); Harold D. Woodman, *New South New Law: The Legal Foundations of the Credit and Labor Relations in the Postbellum*

Agricultural South (Baton Rouge: Louisiana State University Press, 1995); Gavin Wright, *Old South, New South: Revolutions in the Southern Economy Since the Civil War* (New York: Basic Books, 1986).

5. Frederick Bode and Donald Ginter, *Farm Tenancy and the Census in Antebellum Georgia* (Athens: University of Georgia Press, 1986), introduction.

6. Ibid., 90.

7. Steven Hahn, *The Roots of Southern Populism: Yeomen Farmers and the Transformation of the Georgia Upcountry, 1850–1890* (New York: Oxford University Press, 1983), 74.

8. Ibid., 156 and 159.

9. Woodman, *New South, New Law*, 67–94 and Foner, *Reconstruction*, 565–601.

10. Pete Daniel, *Breaking the Land: The Transformation of Cotton, Tobacco and Rice Cultures since 1880* (Urbana: University of Illinois Press, 1985), 15–16, 22.

11. Pete Daniel, *Standing at the Crossroads: Southern Life in the Twentieth Century* (New York: Hill and Wang, 1986), 11–12.

12. United States Census Office, *Tenth Census of The United States: 1880; Eleventh Census of the United States: 1890; Twelfth Census of the United States: 1900; Thirteenth Census of the United States: 1910; Fourteenth Census of the United States: 1920; Fifteenth Census of the United States: 1930.*

13. United States Census Office, *Thirteenth Census; Fourteenth Census; Fifteenth Census.*

14. United States Census Office, *Twelfth Census; Thirteenth Census; Fourteenth Census.*

15. Roy Talbert, Jr., *FDR's Utopian: Arthur Morgan of the TVA* (Jackson: University Press of Mississippi, 1987), 9, 22–23.

16. Ibid., 25–27.

17. H. L. Mitchell, *Mean Things Happen in this Land: The Life and Times of H. L. Mitchell, Co-founder of the Southern Tenant Farmer's Union* (Montclair: Allanheld, Osmun & Co. Publishers, Inc., 1979), 25.

18. H. L. Mitchell, *The Official Papers of the Southern Tenant Farmer's Union* [Hereafter cited as STFU] (Ann Arbor: University Microfilms, 1973), November 30, 1972.

19. Ibid.,; United States Census Office, *Thirteenth Census; Fourteenth Census; Fifteenth Census.*

20. Howard Kester, 1934 Report. *Kester Papers*, Reel one.

21. "Social and Economic Consequences of the Cotton Reduction Program," *Norman Thomas Papers, 1904–1967* (Alexandria, Va.: Chadwyck-Healey, 1983), Reel fifty-nine, 4. [Hereafter cited as *Norman Thomas Papers.*]

22. Ibid., 3.

23. New York World Telegram, July 30, 1935 *Southern Tenant Farmers Union Scrapbook and Newspaper Clippings, 1934–1970* (Chapel Hill: University of North Carolina Library, 1971–1973), Reel A. [Hereafter cited as Scrapbook.]

24. Daniel, *Standing at the Crossroads*, 11–12.

25. Ibid., 12.

26. Thomas D. Clark, *The Emerging South* (New York: Oxford University Press, 1961), 40–56 and *The Statistical History of the United States from Colonial Times to the Present* (Stamford: Fairfield Publishers, Inc., 1965), 301–302.

27. *Statistical History of the United States*, 301–302.

28. Clark, *The Emerging South*, 41–42.

29. United States Census Office, *Fourteenth Census; Fifteenth Census.*

30. Donald Holley, *Uncle Sam's Farmers: The New Deal Communities in the Lower Mississippi Valley* (Urbana: University of Illinois Press, 1975), 11.

31. William Faulkner, *The Wild Palms* (New York: Vintage Books, 1966), 63–64.

32. Granville Whittiker, interview by Jim Ross, tape recording, August 1992.

33. The National Emergency Council, *Report on Economic Condition of the South* (Washington D. C.: Government Printing Office, 1938), 15; Holly, *Uncle Sam's Farmers*, 11.

34. Donald Crichton Alexander, *The Arkansas Plantation: 1920–1942* (New Haven: Yale University Press, 1943), 24.

35. *Statistical History of the United States*, 301–302.

36. Alexander, *The Arkansas Plantation*, 25.

37. Daniel, *Standing at the Crossroads*, 11–12.

38. Alexander, *The Arkansas Plantation*, 25–29; Donald Holley, "The Plantation Heritage: Agriculture in the Arkansas Delta," in Jeannie Whayne and Willard B. Gatewood, ed. *The Arkansas Delta: Land of Paradox*, 261.

39. United States Census Office, *Fifteenth Census; Sixteenth Census of the United States.*

40. Dale Maharidge and Michael Williamson, *And Their Children after Them* (New York: Pantheon Books, 1989), xv-xix.

41. C. Horace Hamilton, "The Social Effects of Recent Trends in the Mechanization of Agriculture," *Rural Sociology* (March, 1939).

42. Pete Daniel, *Standing at the Crossroads: Southern Life in the Twentieth Century* (New York: Hill & Wang, 1986), 120–124.

43. Samuel I. Rosenman, ed., *The Public Papers and Addresses of Franklin D. Roosevelt*, vol. 1 (New York: Random House, 1938), 646.

44. Rosenman, *The Public Papers and Addresses*, vol. 2, 74. By February 1933 the purchasing power of farmers had fallen to fifty percent of what it had been before the World War. Theodore Saloutos, *The American Farmer and the New Deal* (Ames, Iowa: The Iowa State University Press, 1982), 48.

45. Saloutos, *The American Farmer*, 48.

46. Rosenman, *The Public Papers and Addresses*, vol., 2, 258–259. Total expenditure for 1933 was $110,000,000.00

47. H. L. Mitchell, *Mean Things Happening*, 42.

48. Howard Kester, *Revolt Among the Sharecroppers* (New York: Arno Press, Inc., 1969 [1936]), 26.

49. Mitchell, *Mean Things Happening* 41–43; Saloutos, *The American Farmer* (Ames: The Iowa University Press, 1982), 34–49.

CHAPTER TWO

1. Jerold S. Auerbach, "Southern Tenant Farmers: Socialist Critics of the New Deal." *Labor History* 7 (Winter, 1966), 2–22; David Boling, "Sharecroppers for Civil Liberties" *Southern Historian* 10 (1989); Louis Cantor, A *Prologue to the Protest Movement* (Durham: Duke University Press, 1969); David Eugene Conrad, *The Forgotten Farmer: The Story of Sharecroppers in the New Deal* (Urbana: University of Illinois Press, 1965); Donald H. Grubbs, Cry *From the Cotton: The Southern Tenant Farmers' Union and the New Deal* (Chapel Hill: The University of North Carolina Press, 1971); Howard Kester, *Revolt Among The Sharecroppers* (New York: Arno Press, 1969); H. L. Mitchell, Mean *Things Happening in this Land: The Life and Times of H. L. Mitchell Co-founder of the Southern Tenant Farmers' Union* (Montclair: Allanheld, Osmun., 1979); Mark D. Naison, "The Southern Tenant Farmers' Union and the CIO," *Radical America* 2 (1968) 36–56; M. S. Venkataramani, "Norman Thomas, Arkansas Sharecroppers, and the Roosevelt Agricultural Policies, 1933–1937" *Mississippi Valley Historical Review* 47 (September 1960) 3–28; Jeannie M. Whayne, A

New Plantation South: Land, Labor, and Federal Favor in Twentieth-Century Arkansas (Charlottesville: University Press of Virginia, 1996).

2. Howard Kester, *Revolt of the Sharecroppers* (New York: Arno Press, 1969) 54–59.

3. I am not suggesting that Mitchell lied; he was simply attempting to create his own historical memory.

4. H. L. Mitchell, *Mean Things Happening in this Land: The Life and Times of H. L. Mitchell Co-founder of the Southern Tenant Farmers' Union* (Montclair: Allanheld, Osmun, 1979) 4; Sue Thrasher and Leah Wise, *No More Moanin' Voices of the Southern Struggle* (Chapel Hill: The Institute for Southern Studies, 1974.) 13; and H.L. Mitchell, "My Life in Small Town America," Speech given at Boise State University December 1, 1975. *The Green Rising, 1910–1977: A Supplement to the Southern Tenant Farmers' Union Papers*. [Hereafter: *Green Rising*] (Glen Rock, NJ: Microfilming Corporation of America, 1978), Reel eight.

5. Mitchell, *Mean Things* 19; Thrasher, *No More Moanin'*, 13; Mitchell, "My Life in Small Town America"; and H. L. Mitchell, "1941 Manuscript," *Green Rising*, Reel one.

6. Ibid.

7. Mitchell, "1941 Manuscript, " *Green Rising*, Reel one.

8. Mitchell, "My Life in Small Town America," 6–7. *Green Rising*, Reel one.

9. Mitchell, *Mean Things*, 10–11.

10. These categories were found in two "little blue books," *Haldeman-Julius Publications* (Girard, Kansas USA) and *Catalogue of 700 Large Books*. No date of publication.

11. Mitchell, "My Life in Small Town America," 5, *Green Rising*, Reel eight, and Mitchell, "1941 Manuscript," 11 *Green Rising*, Reel one.

12. Mitchell, "My Life in Small Town America," 8–9, *Green Rising*, Reel eight.

13. Mitchell, "1941 Manuscript," 3, *Green Rising*, Reel one.

14. See claim in Mitchell, *Mean Things*, 11–14.

15. Mitchell, "My Life in Small Town America," 5, *Green Rising*, Reel eight.

16. Mitchell, "1941 Manuscript," 11, *Green Rising*, Reel one.

17. Mitchell, "My Life in Small Town America," 5, *Green Rising*, Reel eight, and Mitchell, "1941 Manuscript," 11–12, *Green Rising*, Reel one.

18. Mitchell, *Mean Things*, 17.

19. Mitchell, *Mean Things*, 13, and Whayne, *A New Plantation South*, 187.

20. Mitchell, *Mean Things*, 22.

21. Mitchell, *Mean Things*, 22–23, and Thrasher, *Southern Exposure*, 13.

22. Grubbs, *Cry From the Cotton*, 27.

23. Thrasher, *No More Moanin'*, 13; Clay East, interviewed by H. L. Mitchell, November 27, 1971, *Green Rising*, Reel three.

24. *Marked Tree Tribune*. April 22, 1927.

25. Mitchell, *Mean Things*, 27; J. R. Butler, interviewed by H. L. Mitchell, April 15, 1975 *Green Rising*, Reel seven.

26. Mitchell, *Mean Things*, 27; Thrasher, *No More Moanin'*, 14, and Clay East Interview, *Green Rising*, Reel three, 1971.

27. Grubbs, *Cry From the Cotton*, 27; James R. Green, *Grass-Roots Socialism: Radical Movements in the Southwest, 1895–1943* (Baton Rouge: Louisiana State University Press, 1978) 415; Mitchell, *Mean Things*, 27–28.

28. Mitchell, *Mean Things*, 31; "The Reminiscence of H. L. Mitchell 1956," *Green Rising*, Reel ten.

29. Mitchell, *Mean Things*, 31; Thrasher, *No More Moanin'*, 14. Joe East, interviewed by H. L. Mitchell, April 16, 1975, *Green Rising*, Reel seven; and Clay East interviewed by H. L . Mitchell, *Green Rising*, Reel three, 1971.

30. Phillip S. Foner, *We, the Other People: Alternative Declarations of Independence by Labor Groups, Farmers, Women's' Rights Advocates, Socialists, and Blacks 1829–1975* (Urbana: University of Illinois Press, 1976) 155.

31. Mitchell, *Mean Things*, 33, and J. R. Butler, interviewed by H. L. Mitchell, *Green Rising*, Reel seven, 13.

32. *Theodore Draper Papers*, Box 16, Folder 11, Socialist party.

33. David A. Shannon, *The Socialist Party of America: A History* (Chicago: Quadrangle Books, 1955) 211–215 ; W. A. Swanberg, *Norman Thomas: The Last Idealist* (New York: Charles Scribner's Sons, 1976) 115; and J. R. Butler, interview, *Green Rising*, Reel seven, 14–15.

34. Mitchell, *Mean Things*, 32.

35. H. L. Mitchell, "There Are Mean Things Happening in this Land," *Green Rising*, Reel ten, 36. This is an early version of Mitchell's autobiography.

36. Ibid. It is interesting that when these notes were finally made into a book this remembrance of his own youthful radicalism was deleted.

37. Green, *Grass-Roots Socialism*, 18, and Elliot Shore, *Talkin' Socialism: J. A. Wayland and the Role of the Press in American Radicalism, 1890–1912* (Lawrence: The University of Kansas, 1988) 1–93 and 221–222.

38. Martha B. Johnson to Norman Thomas, November 9, 1933, *Green Rising*, Reel one.

39. H. L. Mitchell to Gardner Jackson, September 3, 1936, STFU Reel three; Jerold S. Auerbach, "The Organizing Drive of the Southern Tenant Farmers' Union In Arkansas" paper delivered at the Southern Historical Association November 13, 1964, in *Norman Thomas Papers*, Reel fifty-nine; Memorandum from H.L Mitchell to Norman Thomas, *Norman Thomas Papers*, Reel fifty-nine; H. L. Mitchell to Jerold Auerbach, November 24, 1964; Jerold Auerbach to H L. Mitchell, February 2, 1965, STFU *Papers*, Reel fifty.

40. On the Communist Party in the "Third Period," see Irving Bernstein, *The Lean Years: A History of the American Worker, 1920–1933* (New York: Da Capo Press, Inc., 1960), 20–28; John Patrick Diggins, *The Rise and Fall of the American Left* (New York: W. W. Norton and Company, 1992), 146–154; Theodore Draper, *American Communism and Soviet Russia* (New York: Vintage Books, 1960), 302–306; Irving Howe and Lewis Coser, *The American Communist Party: A Critical History* (New York: Frederick A. Praeger, Pub., 1957), 188–197;*Maurice Isserman, Which Side Were You On?: The American Communist Party During the Second World War* (Urbana: University of Illinois Press, 1993), 3–4; Harvey Klehr, *The Heyday of American Communism: The Depression Decade* (New York: Basic Books, 1984), 8–17; Fraser M. Ottanelli, *The Communist Party of the United States: From the Depression to World War II* (New Brunswick: Rutgers University Press, 1991), 17–22.

41. A good discussion of radicalism in the 1930s appears in Milton Cantor, *The Divided Left: American Radicalism, 1900–1975* (New York: Hill and Wang, 1978), Chapter 6. On the Socialist party see books already mentioned and Norman Thomas, *As I See It* (New York: Macmillan Company, 1932).

42. Clay East to H. L. Mitchell, January 27, 1970, STFU *Papers*, Reel fifty-seven; William Amberson to Norman Thomas, August 24, 1934; Norman Thomas to William Amberson August 28 1934; and Thomas to H. L. Mitchell, August 28, 1934, *Green Rising*, Reel One.

43. This sectarianism found expression in his work with Commonwealth College and Communist leaders in the United Cannery, Agricultural, Packing and Allied Workers of America.

44. Foner, *We, the Other People*, 156–158.

45. Although the Communist Party had organized Unemployment Leagues, by 1933–34 non-Communist groups were using the leagues to organize the unemployed.

On Unemployment Leagues, see Foner, *We, the Other People*, 159–162; Mitchell, *Mean Things*, 35; and Whayne, *A New Plantation South*, 187–189.

46. Mitchell, "There Are Mean Things," 37–38, *Green Rising*, Reel ten.

47. Mitchell, "There Are Mean Things," 38, *Green Rising*, Reel ten, and "Early Life of H. L. Mitchell," interviewed by Bell I Wiley, 1972, 11–12.

48. Carl H. Moneyhon, *Arkansas and the New South , 1874–1929* (Fayetteville: The University of Arkansas Press, 1997) 78–93. On pre-socialist radicalism see Edward L. Ayers, *The Promise of the New South: Life After Reconstruction* (New York: Oxford University Press, 1992), 45–47 and 215–217; Lawrence Goodwyn, *Democratic Promise: The Populist Movement in America* (New York: Oxford University Press, 1976), 15–17; C. Vann Woodward, *Origins of the New South, 1877–1913* (Baton Rouge: Louisiana State University Press, 1951 [1971]), 83–86.

49. Green, *Grass-Roots Socialism*, 12–52; 126–175.

50. *American Guardian*, February 1934

51. Roy Reed, *Faubus: The Life and Times of An American Prodigal* (Fayetteville: The University of Arkansas Press, 1997), 25–40; Green, *Grass-Roots Socialism*, Chapters IV and VI; Carl H. Moneyhon, *Arkansas and the New South*, 61–93, 116; G. Gregory Kiser. "The Socialist Party in Arkansas, 1900–1912," *Arkansas Historical Quarterly* 40 (Summer 1981): 119–53.

52. Martha Johnson to Thomas, November 9, 1933 and Norman Thomas to Martha Johnson, November 16, 1933, *Green Rising*, Reel one.

53. *Sharecroppers Voice*, November 1935, "Clayton Taylor Held in Jail," H. L. Mitchell, STFU *Papers*, Reel one.

54. "Deplores Lot of Southern Tenants: Norman Thomas Says a Bear in a Zoo is in Luck By Comparison," *Arkansas Gazette*, February 18, 1934.

55. Mitchell, *Mean Things*, 39.

56. The story of the visit and Norman Thomas' speech is reconstructed from the *Arkansas Gazette*, February 18, 1934; *American Guardian*, February 1934, *Scrapbook*, Reel A.; "Thomas Charge Elicits Report from Johnston: AAA Official says Government will Protect Tenant From Owner's Mistreatment" Clipping with No Paper Name, February 19, 1934, *Scrapbook*, Reel A; *Arkansas Gazette*, "Norman Thomas, Socialist, will speak at Tyronza Today" February 17, 1934; *Memphis Commercial Appeal*, February 1934.

57. William Amberson to H. L. Mitchell Feb 22, 1934 University of Memphis Special Collections, *William Amberson Papers*; H. L. Mitchell to Eddie Johnson,

February 22, 1934; Norman Thomas to H. L. Mitchell, March 26, 1934, *Green Rising*, Reel one.

58. William Amberson Biography from *Amberson Papers*, "Scope and Content" University of Memphis; William Amberson to Norman Thomas, March 31, 1939, STFU *Papers*, Reel three.

59. Amberson to Norman Thomas, February 22, 1934, *Green Rising*, Reel one.

60. Mitchell to Norman Thomas, February 21, 1934, *Green Rising*, Reel one.

61. Memphis Commercial Appeal, "Erroneous" *Memphis Commercial Appeal*, February 1934

62. *Press Scimitar*, February 19, 1934.

63. Clay East to Oscar Johnston, February 19, 1934, *Scrapbook*, Reel A.

64. Oscar Johnston to Clay East and H. L Mitchell, February 20, 1934, *Scrapbook*, Reel A.

65. H. L. Mitchell to Oscar Johnston March 1, 1934, *Green Rising*, Reel one.

66. *Parkin Times* (Parkin Arkansas), February 23 1934.

67. *Arkansas Gazette*, February 20, 1934

68. George Morris to Norman Thomas, March 8, 1934, *Green Rising*, Reel one.

69. John C. Stevens to Norman Thomas, March 12, 1934, *Green Rising*, Reel one.

70. George Parke to Norman Thomas, March 11, 1934, *Green Rising*, Reel one.

71. Norman Thomas to Editor, March 3, 1934; Norman Thomas to Asheville Citizen, March 6, 1934; Norman Thomas to Assistant Publisher, March 15, 1935, *Green Rising*, Reel one.

72. Norman Thomas to H. L. Mitchell, April 9, 1934; Lois Bray to Norman Thomas, April 6, 1934, and Ed Wilson to Norman Thomas, April 15, 1934, *Green Rising*, Reel one.

73. Norman Thomas to Henry Wallace, February 22, 1934, *Green Rising*, Reel one.

74. Graham White and John Maze. *Wallace: Henry A. Wallace His Search For a New World Order* (Chapel Hill: University of North Carolina Press, 1995) 44–56; Theodore Salutos, *The American Farmer and the New Deal* (Ames: Iowa University Press, 1982) 34–49.

75. Henry Wallace to Marvin H. McIntyre, Assistant Secretary to the President, March 3, 1934, *Wallace Papers at the University of Iowa* (Iowa City: University of Iowa Libraries, 1974), Reel nineteen.

76. Henry Wallace to Norman Thomas, March 8, 1934, *Green Rising*, Reel one; Henry Wallace to Edward J, Meehen, March 13, 1934, *Wallace Papers*, Reel nineteen; Henry Wallace to Norman Thomas, May 14, 1934, *Green Rising*, Reel one.

77. Clay East to Editor of the *Press-Scimitar*, February 25, 1934, *Clay East Papers*, Universtiy of Arkansas Special Collections.

78. "Cobb Probing Charges of Sharecropper Evictions: Landowner Explains Why Boston was Ordered to Leave Tyronza Farm" *Press Scimitar*, March 1934, Scrapbook A.

79. H. L. Mitchell to Norman Thomas, March 11, 1934, *Green Rising*, Reel one.

80. Telegram from Norman Thomas to Henry Wallace, March 10, 1934, *Green Rising*, Reel one.

81. Telegraph from Norman Thomas to William Amberson, March 10, 1934; Norman Thomas to Martha B. Johnson March 14, 1934, *Green Rising*, Reel one.

82. *New York Times*, March 11, 1934, Section II, p.2:4.

83. Telegram William Amberson to Norman Thomas, March 12, 1934, *Norman Thomas Papers*, Reel fifty-nine; Jack Temple Kirby, *Rural Worlds Lost* (Baton Rouge: Louisiana University Press, 1987), 60–61; Paul E. Mertz, *New Deal Policy and Southern Rural Poverty* (Baton Rouge: Louisiana State Universtiy Press, 1978), 40–41; Bruce J. Schulman, *From Cotton Belt to Sunbelt: Federal Policy, Economic Development, and the Transformation of the South, 1938–1980* (New York: Oxford University Press, 1991), 16.

84. AP story found in the *Norman Thomas Papers*, Reel fifty-nine.

85. Telegraph Paul Appelby to Norman Thomas, March 12,1934, Newspaper Clippings from March 1934, *Norman Thomas Papers*, Reel fifty-nine; H. l. Mitchell to Norman Thomas, March 20, 1934, *Green Rising*, Reel one.

86. "Says Investigation of Tenant Conditions was Superficial," *Arkansas Gazette*, March 21, 1934; H. L. Mitchell, "Land Bosses of Arkansas Whitewashed," *American Guardian*, March 1934, found in the *Norman Thomas Papers*, Reel fifty-nine.

87. H. L. Mitchell to Norman Thomas, March 20, 1934, *Green Rising*, Reel one.

88. *Arkansas Gazette*, March 21, 1934.

CHAPTER THREE

1. Mitchell, *Mean Things*, 40; H. L. Mitchell to Norman Thomas, March 11, 1934, *Green Rising*, Reel one; H. L. Mitchell to Norman Thomas, February 21, 1934, *Green Rising*, Reel one; "Wonderful People I have known," Speech by H. L. Mitchell 1971, *Green Rising*, Reel three.

2. H. L. Mitchell to Norman Thomas, March 25, 1934, *Green Rising*, Reel one.

3. H. L. Mitchell to Norman Thomas, April 12, 1934, *Green Rising*, Reel one.

4. H. L. Mitchell to Norman Thomas, March 25, 1934 and April 12, 1934, *Green Rising*, Reel one.

5. H. L. Mitchell to Norman Thomas April 4, 1934, *Green Rising*, Reel one; Norman Thomas to Clay East, April 9, 1934; H. L. Mitchell to Norman Thomas, April 12, 1934; *The Marked Tree Tribune* of January 28, 1927 reported that East's father and brother had moved to Miami, Arizona; Clay East to Norman Thomas, June 1, 1934, *Green Rising*, Reel one.

6. "Recollections of Storm Center Rodgers, 1932–1976" interview with Ward Rodgers, April 30, 1976, *Green Rising*, Reel eight.

7. H. L. Mitchell to Norman Thomas, April 15, 1934; Norman Thomas to H. L. Mitchell, April 17, 1934; Clark Waldron to Thomas, April 28, 1934; William Amberson to Norman Thomas, May 4, 1934; Norman Thomas to H. L. Mitchell, May 11, 1934; Norman Thomas to Clark Waldron, May 11, 1934, *Green Rising*, Reel one.

8. William Amberson to Norman Thomas February 22, 1934, *Green Rising*, Reel one.

9. William Amberson to Clarence Senior, March 1, 1934, University of Memphis Special Collections, *William Amberson Papers*.

10. William Amberson to Norman Thomas, March 4, 1934, *Green Rising*, Reel one.

11. Ibid.

12. William Amberson to Norman Thomas, March 29, 1934, *Green Rising*, Reel one.

13. William Amberson to Norman Thomas, April 2, 1934; William Amberson to Norman Thomas, April 15, 1934; Clark Waldron to Norman Thomas, April 16, 1934, *Green Rising*, Reel one.

14. William Amberson to Norman Thomas, April 2, 1934; William Amberson to Thomas, April 14, 1934; Clark Waldron to Norman Thomas, April 16, 1934; Norman Thomas to William Amberson, April 10, 1934, *Green Rising*, Reel one.

15. William Amberson to Norman Thomas, March 29, 1934; Norman Thomas to William Amberson, April 2, 1934; " The Social and Economic Consequences of the Cotton Acreage Reduction Program," in *Norman Thomas Papers*, Reel fifty-nine.

16. Report found in the William Amberson papers, no date.

17. "The Social and Economic" *Norman Thomas Papers*, Reel fifty-nine.

18. Norman Thomas to William Amberson, May 10, 1934, and Norman Thomas to Clark Waldron, May 11, 1935, *Green Rising*, Reel one.

19. Martha Johnson to Norman Thomas July 11, 1934, and Norman Thomas to Martha Johnson, July 20, 1934, *Norman Thomas Papers*, Reel fifty-nine.

20. Clay East to Norman Thomas, June 1, 1934, *Norman Thomas Papers*, Reel fifty-nine; Norman Thomas to H. L. Mitchell, June 21, 1934; H. L. Mitchell to Norman Thomas, July 14, 1934; Norman Thomas to William Amberson, May 10, 1934; Norman Thomas To Clark Waldron, May 11, 1934, *Green Rising*, Reel one.

21. Norman Thomas to H. L. Mitchell, June 21, 1934, *Green Rising*, Reel one.

22. Martha Johnson to H. L. Mitchell, July 11, 1934, *Norman Thomas Papers*, Reel fifty-nine.

23. Norman Thomas to William Amberson, March 31, 1939, STFU *Papers*, Reel three.

24. Norman Thomas to H. L. Mitchell, March 26, 1934; Norman Thomas to William Amberson, April 2, 1934; Norman Thomas to H. l. Mitchell, April 9, 1934; Norman Thomas to William Amberson, May 10, 1934; Norman Thomas to Clark Waldron, May 11, 1934, *Green Rising*, Reel one.

25. Clark Waldron to Norman Thomas, April 6, 1934, *Norman Thomas Papers*, Reel fifty-nine; Clark Waldron to William Amberson, *Amberson Papers*; H. L. Mitchell to Norman Thomas, June 8, 1934 *Green Rising*, Reel one; Norman Thomas to H. L. Mitchell, July 9, 1934, *Green Rising*, Reel one.

26. Martha Johnson to H. L. Mitchell, July 11, 1934, *Norman Thomas Papers*, Reel one.

27. H. L. Mitchell to Norman Thomas, July 1934, *Green Rising*, Reel one.

28. Norman Thomas to Martha Johnson, July 20, 1934, *Norman Thomas Papers*, Reel fifty-nine; William Amberson to Norman Thomas, *Norman Thomas Papers*, Reel fifty-nine; H. L. Mitchell to Norman Thomas, *Green Rising*, Reel one.

29. There is no evidence that Mitchell or the other socialists knew of the Sharecroppers Union in Alabama until 1935.

30. H. L. Mitchell to Norman Thomas, April 12, 1934, *Green Rising*, Reel one.

31. H.L Mitchell to Norman Thomas, March 25, 1934, *Green Rising*, Reel one; J. Clark Waldron to William Amberson, April 6, 1934, *Green Rising*, Reel one; Mitchell to Norman Thomas, April 12, 1934, *Green Rising*, Reel one; Norman Thomas to H. L Mitchell, July 26, 1934, *Green Rising*, Reel one; Clay East to Norman Thomas June 1, 1934, *Norman Thomas Paper*, Reel fifty-nine.

32. H. L. Mitchell to Norman Thomas, July 4, 1934, *Green Rising*, Reel one.

33. "Outline of Proposed Union," *William Amberson Papers*.

34. William Amberson to Thomas, July 22, 1934, *Norman Thomas Papers*, Reel fifty-nine.

35. Norman Thomas to H. L. Mitchell, July 26, 1934, *Green Rising*, Reel one; William Amberson to Norman Thomas, August 24, 1934, *Green Rising*, Reel one; News Release, September 1934, *Norman Thomas Papers*, Reel fifty-nine.

36. I have constructed the story of the STFU rank and file from the following sources: "Early Days of the STFU" (1941), *Green Rising*, Reel one; Interview with Clay East, November 27, 1971, *Green Rising*, Reel five; interview with H L. Mitchell by Lawrence Goodwyn, January 3, 1974, *Green Rising*, Reel five.

37. On violence in the South see: Harry Crews. *A Childhood: The biography of a Place* (New York: Quill, 1983), 7–8; Wayne Flynt. *Poor But Proud: Alabama's Poor Whites* (Tuscaloosa: The University of Alabama Press, 1989), 217; and Robin D. G. Kelly. *Hammer and Hoe: Alabama Communists During the Great Depression* (Chapel Hill: The University of North Carolina Press, 1990), 40–41.

38. H. L. Mitchell, "Early days of the STFU," *Green Rising*, Reel one.

39. H. L. Mitchell to Howard Kester; Clay East to H. L. Mitchell, June 9, 1976, *Green Rising*, Reel eight.

40. Clay East to Mitchell, January 1967, *STFU Papers*, Reel fifty-three; Rodgers interview, April 30, 1976, *Green Rising*, Reel eight; "Early Days of the STFU."

41. H. L. Mitchell to William Amberson, July 25, 1934, *Green Rising*, Reel one.

42. Early Days; "Race Relations in the STFU." Speech, April 4, 1975, *Green Rising*, Reel five; interview Clay East, April 26, 1974, *Green Rising*, Reel six; Mitchell interview by Lawrence Goodwyn, January 29, 1974, *Green Rising*, Reel three; "Wonderful People I've Known in My Lifetime," Speech, 1971, *Green Rising*, Reel three; East Interview, November 27, 1971, *Green Rising*, Reel three; Rodgers interview, April 30, 1976, *Green Rising*, Reel eight.

CHAPTER FOUR

1. Numbers 33.53.

2. Granville Whittiker, interview by Jim Ross, tape recording, August 1992.

3. T. J. Woofter, Jr., *Landlord and Tenant on the Cotton Plantation* (Washington D.C.: Works Progress Administration, 1936), 102.

4. *The Disinherited Speak*, 3, STFU Reel two. When I showed this letter to Issac

Shaw's son in 1992, he told me that he believed that the man in Shaw's story had to be Shaw himself. Shaw's son reported that even in the 1940s Issac Shaw was forced by poverty to bring home strange and suspect food to support his family. I have left all quotes from the sharecroppers and tenant farmers in their original form without the obtrusive "sic."

5. J. L. Lynn to H. L. Mitchell, Truman, Arkansas, January 14, 1936, STFU Reel one.

6. *The Disinherited Speak*, 3, STFU Reel two, and Will Washington to H. L. Mitchell, January 28, 1936, STFU Reel one.

7. John Robinson to H. L. Mitchell, February 18, 1936, STFU Reel one.

8. Clara Jones to H. L. Mitchell, June 13, 1936, STFU Reel two.

9. Ammie Love To H. L. Mitchell, August 12, 1937, STFU Reel Five, and Nathen Wiley to H. L. Mitchell, no date, STFU Reel one.

10. Charlie and Rosie Clayton to H. L. Mitchell, August 9, 1935, STFU Reel one.

11. Mary Lee Moore to Union, December 19, 1935, STFU Reel one.

12. Anonymous to H. L. Mitchell, March 15, 1937, STFU Reel four.

13. Etia Glen to H.L. Mitchell, January 3, 1938, STFU Reel seven.

14. Affidavit of William Stultz, Parkin, Arkansas, June 27, 1935, STFU Reel one.

15. Henry Peters to H. L. Mitchell, January 20, 1936, STFU Reel one.

16. Clayton Thompson to H. L. Mitchell, August 4, 1937, STFU Reel five.

17. Hays Perry to H. L. Mitchell, August 2, 1938, STFU Reel five.

18. *U.S. Department of Commerce, Fourteenth Census of the United States:* 1920, *Agriculture* (Washington D. C. Government Printing Office, 1922), 131.

19. Member 28559 to Headquarters of the Union, March 15, 1937, STFU Reel four.

20. "Disinherited Speak," 7, STFU Reel four.

21. Ibid.

22. Ibid.

23. Member 28559 to Headquarters of the Union, March 15, 1937, STFU Reel four.

24. *The Disinherited Speak*, 19, STFU Reel four.

25. Abe Glen to H. L. Mitchell, January 3, 1937, STFU Reel four.

26. C. J. Spaulding to H. L. Mitchell, August 14, 1937, STFU Reel five.

27. C. J. Spaulding to H. L. Mitchell, August 26, 1937, STFU Reel five.

28. Earl Hollis to H. L. Mitchell, August 28, 1937, STFU Reel five.

29. Nelson Parker to H. L. Mitchell, January 8, 1936, STFU Reel one.

30. Elizabeth Pettigrue to H. L. Mitchell, April 16, 1936, STFU Reel two.

31. Roger L. Ransom and Richard Sutch, *One Kind of Freedom: The Economic Consequences of Emancipation* (Cambridge: Cambridge University Press, 1977), 81.

32. Eric Foner, *Reconstruction: America's Unfinished Revolution, 1863–1877* (New York: Harper and Row, Publishers, 1988), 104; Phillip Foner, *Proceedings of the Black National and State Conventions, 1865–1900* (Philadelphia: Temple University Press) 88; Joseph P. Reidy, *From Slavery to Agrarian Capitalism in the Cotton Plantation South: Central Georgia, 1800–1880* (Chapel Hill: The University of North Carolina Press, 1992), 142 and 195; Roger L. Ransom and Richard Sutch, *One Kind of Freedom,* 81; Julie Saville, *The Work of Reconstruction: From Slave to Wage Laborer in South Carolina, 1860–1870,* (New York: Cambridge University Press, 1994), 96.

33. Quoted in Roger L. Ransom and Richard Sutch, *One Kind of Freedom,* 81.

34. Willard Sterne Randall, *Thomas Jefferson: A Life* (New York: Henry Holt and Company, 1993), 119.

35. Steven Hahn, *The Roots of Southern Populism: Yeoman Farmers and the Transformation of the Georgia Upcountry, 1850–1890* (New York: Oxford University Press, 1983), 29, 40, Chapter 2 passim.

36. "Resolution adopted by the Beth Council at Marked Tree," March 6, 1935, STFU Reel one.

37. Andrew Ice to H. L. Mitchell, January 1939, STFU Reel ten.

38. Chester Wright to H. L. Mitchell, September 28, 1935, STFU Reel one.

39. Austin Williams to H. L. Mitchell, October 21, 1935, STFU Reel one.

40. J. W. Washington to H. L. Mitchell, November 27, 1935, STFU Reel one.

41. "Questionnaire on Rehabilitation," STFU Reel one.

42. William Johnson to J. R. Butler, January 7, 1936, STFU Reel one.

43. W. G. Wellshad to H. L. Mitchell, January 17, 1938, STFU Reel seven.

44. George Bostick to H. L. Mitchell, February 30, 1938, STFU Reel seven.

45. Lula Parchman to H. L. Mitchell, April 5, 1936, STFU Reel two.

46. Ibid.

47. Irvine Nickerson to Unknown, January 1939, STFU Reel ten.

48. H. L. Mitchell to J. W. Heller, January 15, 1936 STFU Reel one.

49. Of course not all these men and women were good family men. There is no need to romanticize these men and women to understand their plight.

50. Howard Kester, "Religion-Priestly and Prophetic in the South," *Radical Religion* (1936): 23–31.

51. Anthony Dunbar, *Against the Grain: Southern Radicals and Prophets, 1929–1959* (Charlottesville: University Press of Virginia, 1981) and Robert F. Martin, *Howard Kester and the Struggle for Social Justice in the South, 1904–77* (Charlottesville: University of Virginia Press, 1991).

52. On the origins of this uniformity see Wayne Flynt, "One in the Spirit, Many in the Flesh: Southern Evangelicals" in David E. Harrell, Jr., ed., *Varieties of Southern Evangelicalism* (Macon: Mercer University Press, 1981).

53. No sharecropper or tenant farmer wrote to the union to express their view of baptism or whether or not there should be clapping in church. In no interview that I have done was anyone concerned with these issues. This leads me to believe that the issues that divided Protestant sects were more important for the ministers. The person in the pew, tended to be more concerned with pleasing Jesus, or praying for relief from sin, suffering, or oppression.

54. Interview Ida Davis, interview by Jim Ross, tape recording August, 1983.

55. For other uses of broad principles in Southern evangelicalism see Jacquelyn Dowd Hall, et al, *Like a Family: the Making of a Southern Cotton Mill World* (Chapel Hill: The University of North Carolina Press, 1987), 175–179; Pete Daniel, *Standing at the Crossroads: Southern Life in the Twentieth Century* (New York: Hill and Wang, 1986), 8.

56. Robert L. Hall and Carol B. Stack, ed., *Holding on to the Land and the Lord: Kinship, Ritual, Land Tenure, and Social Policy in the Rural South* (Athens: The University of Georgia Press, 1982); Pete Daniel, *Standing at the Crossroads*; Jacqulyn Dowd Hall, *Like a Family*; Wayne Flynt, "One in Spirit."

57. N. C. Dickens to H. L. Mitchell and J. R. Butler, January 9, 1937, STFU Reel five, and J. R. Butler to Lula Parchman, July 31, 1936, STFU Reel two.

58. "Program of the Second National Convention, January 3–4, 1936, STFU Reel one.

59. H. L. Mitchell to J. W. Ford, January 11, 1936, STFU Reel one, and Joshua 18:1.

60. M. T. Walton to H. L. Mitchell, January 10, 1936; Ida Jefferson to H. L. Mitchell, January 1936; Henry F. Keys to H. L Mitchell, January 10, 1936; and Dinah Bennett to H., L. Mitchell, January 9, 1936, STFU Reel one.

61. Lula McDonald to H. L. Mitchell, February 11, 1936, STFU Reel one.

62. J. W. Washington to H. L. Mitchell, January 19, 1936, STFU Reel one.

63. A. T. Williams to H. L. Mitchell, February 5, 1937, *STFU* Reel four.

64. Rosie Cline to H. L. Mitchell, 1937 or 1938, *STFU* Reel six.

65. Luke 10.25–37.

66. "The Southern Tenant Framers' Union Forever," *STFU* Reel six.

67. Pronounced "Sice."

68. Stephen Seys to Southern Tenant Farmers Union, no date, *STFU* Reel four.

69. Stephen Seys to STFU, May 1937, *STFU* Reel four.

70. Stephen Seys to STFU, No Date, *STFU* Reel four.

71. Stephen Seys to STFU, April 5, 1937, *STFU* Reel four.

72. Stephen Seys to STFU, May 1937, *STFU* Reel four.

73. Stephen Seys to STFU, No date, *STFU* Reel four.

74. Ibid.

75. Ibid.

76. Stephen Seys to STFU, May 1937, *STFU* Reel four.

77. Ibid.

78. Stephen Seys to STFU, April 5, 1937, *STFU* Reel four.

79. Stephen Seys to STFU, No Date, *STFU* Reel four.

80. Stephen Seys to STFU, No Date, *STFU* Reel four.

81. Stephen Seys to STFU, May 1937, *STFU* Reel four.

82. Ibid.

83. S.C. Seys to STFU, Feb. 6, 1937, *STFU* Reel four.

84. Stephen Seys to STFU, April 5, 1937, *STFU* Reel four.

85. Ibid.

CHAPTER FIVE

1. Henderson Bently to J. R. Butler, February 18, 1937, *STFU* Reel nine.

2. Michael Harrington, forward in *Mean Things Happening in this Land*, ix-x.

3. Edward L. Ayers, *The Promise of the New South: Life After Reconstruction* (New York: Oxford University Press, 1992), 155.

4. C. Vann Woodward, *Origins of the New South, 1877–1913* (Baton Rouge: Louisiana State University Press, 1990 [1951]), 159–60.

5. H. L. Mitchell to Howard Kester, November 29, 1934, *Kester Papers*, Reel one; Affidavit of Arthur Brookings, June 1935, *STFU* Reel one.

6. Mitchell, *Mean Things Happening*, 81–83.

7. Anna Damon to J. Marion Futrell, February 2, 1935, *Futrell Papers*, 407,

Commonwealth College; Mrs. T. P. Martin to Norman Thomas, April 1, 1935, *Green Rising*, Reel one; H. L. Mitchell to Jack Herling, April 1, 1935, *Green Rising*, Reel one; *The Sharecroppers Voice*, May 1935, *Green Rising*, Reel one; Mrs. Ernestine Williams to Norman Thomas, April 7, 1935, *Green Rising*, Reel one.

8. "Why Cotton Pickers Strike," September 1935, STFU Reel one.

9. James Green, *Grass-Roots Socialism*, 424–25.

10. J. E. Cameron to Mitchell, November 23, 1935, STFU Reel one.

11. Anonymous to Mitchell, January 14, 1936, STFU Reel one.

12. H. L. Mitchell, "The Southern Tenant Farmers Union: Third Annual Convention Report," January 14–17, 1937, STFU Reel four; STFU Press Release, January 18, 1936, STFU Reel one.

13. Lester Robinson to Howard Kester, February 10, 1936, *Kester Papers*, Reel two; Charles Fleming to Governor J. Marion Futrell, June 9, 1936, *Futrell Papers*, 432, STFU.

14. Donald H. Grubbs, *Cry From the Cotton*, 117.

15. Dorothy Weaver, interview by Jim Ross, tape recording, August 1992.

16. *Disinherited Speak*, 9, STFU Reel two.

17. Grif Stockley, *Blood In Their Eyes: The Elaine Race Massacres of* 1919 (Fayetteville: The University of Arkansas Press, 2001).

18. H. L. Mitchell to Denver L. Dudley, January 20, 1936, *Futrell Papers*, 431, STFU; J. Marion Futrell to J. T. Robinson, March 10, 1936, *Futrell Papers*, 434, STFU; Press Release from Federal Council of Churches, June 8, 1936, STFU *Reel two*.

19. H. L. Mitchell, "Race Relations in the Southern Tenant Farmers' Union," April 4, 1973, Speech given at Princeton University, *Green Rising*, Reel five.

20. J. R. Butler to W. R. Dyess, June 29, 1935, STFU Reel one.

21. Norman Thomas to Howard Kester and H. L. Mitchell, No Date, STFU Reel three; J. L. Lynn to H. L. Mitchell, February 6, 1936, STFU Reel one.

22. C. T. Carpenter to Norman Thomas, April 27, 1935, *Green Rising*, Reel one; C. T. Carpenter to Norman Thomas, May 11, 1935, *Green Rising*, Reel one; Interview with Sidney Herzberg by H. L. Mitchell November 19, 1975, *Green Rising*, Reel eight; Interview with Clay East, by H. L. Mitchell, November 27, 1971, *Green Rising*, Reel three.

23. Ward Rodger to Norman Thomas, June 18, 1935, *Green Rising*, Reel one; H. L. Mitchell, "A Grass Roots View of the New Deal," January 29, 1974, *Green Rising*, Reel five; Recollections of Storm Center Rodgers, April 30, 1976, *Green Rising*, Reel eight.

24. W. B. Moore to J. R. Butler, May 26, 1937, STFU Reel four.

25. Mitchell, *Mean Things Happening*, 80–81.

26. Gilbert Fite, *Cotton Fields No More: Southern Agriculture, 1865–1980* (Lexington: The University Press of Kentucky, 1984), 153.

27. Ibid., 150–2.

28. Ibid., 151.

29. Pete Daniel, *Breaking the Land: The Transformation of Cotton, Tobacco, and Rice Cultures Since 1880* (Urbana: University of Illinois Press, 1985), 175.

30. C. Horace Hamilton, "Social Effects of Recent Trends in the Mechanization of Agriculture," *Rural Sociology*, 4 (March 1939), 1.

31. Fite, *Cotton Fields No More*, 152.

32. C. Horace Hamilton, "The Social Effects of Recent Trends in the Mechanization of Agriculture." *Rural Sociology* (1939).

33. "The Source of the Grapes of Wrath," H. L. Mitchell, August 14–16, 1940, STFU Reel fifteen.

34. Jerold S. Auerbach, "The Organizing Drive of the Southern Tenant Farmers Union in Arkansas." Unpublished paper delivered at the Southern Historical Association, November 13, 1964, *Norman Thomas Papers*, Reel fifty-nine.

35. Grubs, *Cry From the Cotton*, 66.

36. Leon Turner to H. L. Mitchell, July 19, 1937, STFU Reel five.

37. H. L. Mitchell to J. P. Martain, February 2, 1936, STFU Reel one.

38. Local Secretary's Report, September 1, 1936, STFU Reel three.

39. J. R. Butler to J. F. Hynds, April 1, 1937, STFU Reel four.

40. H. L. Mitchell to E. B. McKinney, April 6, 1936, STFU Reel two; H. L. Mitchell to E. B. McKinney, April 11, 1936, STFU Reel two; E. B. McKinney to H. L. Mitchell, April 11, 1936, STFU Reel two.

41. E. B. McKinney to H. L. Mitchell, April 20, 1936, STFU Reel two; H. L. Mitchell to E. B. McKinney April 22, 1936, STFU Reel two; Sidney Hertzberg to John Handcox, April 16, 1937, STFU Reel four.

42. A. B. Brookins to STFU Executive Council, August 16, 1936, STFU Reel two.

43. Unknown to E. B. McKinney, July 31, 1936, STFU Reel two; H. L. Mitchell to A. B. Brookins, August 20, 1936, STFU Reel two.

44. Report of the National Executive Council Meeting, January 30, 1937, STFU Reel four; E. B. McKinney to J. R. Butler, February 17, 1937 STFU Reel four; J. R. Butler to E. B. McKinney, February 18, 1937, STFU Reel four; E. B. McKinney to H. L. Mitchell, April 29, 1937, STFU Reel four.

45. H. L. Mitchell to unknown, September 26, 1937 *Kester* Reel three.

46. Ibid., H. L. Mitchell to Donald Henderson, September 30, 1937, STFU Reel five.

47. Ibid.

48. *The Southern States Cotton Cropper*, September 1940, *News A*.

49. H. L .Mitchell to Clay East, April 4, 1939, *East Papers*.

50. J. R. Butler to Henderson Bently, STFU Reel nine.

51. On radicalism and socialism see: Oscar Ameringer, *If You Don't Weaken: The Autobiography of Oscar Ameringer* (Norman: The University of Oklahoma Press, 1983); Phillip S. Foner, *The Workingmen's Party of the United States: A History of the First Marxist Party in the Americas* (Minneapolis: MEP Publications, 1984); John Graham, ed., *"Yours For the Revolution:" The Appeal to Reason, 1895–1922* (Lincoln: University of Nebraska Press, 1990); James R. Green, *Grassroots Socialism; Irving* Howe, *Socialism and America* (New York: Harcourt Brace Javanovicah, Publishers, 1985).

52. Foner, *The Workingmen's Party*, 25.

53. James Green, Introduction to Armeringer, *If You Don't Weaken*, xxiii.

54. Green, *Grassroots Socialism*, xi.

55. Lawrence Goodwyn, "The Cooperative Commonwealth and Other Abstractions: In Search of a Democratic Premise," *Marxist Perspectives*, (1980).

56. Graham, *Yours for the Revolution*, 155.

57. Norman Thomas, *America's Way Out: A Program for Democracy* (New York: The Macmillan Company, 1931); *The Choice Before Us* (New York: Arno Press, 1970); *Human Exploitation in the United States* (New York: Frederick A. Stokes Co., 1934).

58. Ibid., "Membership Book," STFU Reel one.

59. STFU, "Report from Executive Committee," November 1934, STFU Reel one.

60. "Constitution of the Southern Tenant Farmers' Union," 1935, STFU Reel one.

61. Holley, *Uncle Sam's Farmers*, 25.

62. J. R. Butler to Colonel Lawrence Westbrook, 1935, STFU Reel one.

63. "Flyer of the Southern Tenant Farmers' Union," 1936, STFU Reel three.

64. Mitchell to unknown, May 21, 1936, STFU Reel three.

65. Green, *Grassroots Socialism*, 427, and Mitchell, *Mean Things Happening*, 86–103.

66. Orville Vernon Burton, "Howard Kester (1 904–77)" in Mari Jo Buhle, Paul Buhle, and Dan Georgakas ed., *Encyclopedia of American Radicalism* (Urbana: University of Illinois Press, 1992), 401–02.

67. Howard Kester, "Testimony Submitted to the Governor's Commission on Farm Tenancy," 1936, *STFU* Reel three.

68. Ibid.

69. Ibid.

70. Kester, *Revolt Among the Sharecroppers*, 91.

71. Ibid.

72. Ibid., 91–92.

73. Ibid., 92.

74. Ibid., 93.

75. Howard Kester, "The Human Side of Cotton Tenancy," December 29, 1936, *STFU* Reel three.

76. Ibid.

77. John C. Cort, *Christian Socialism: An Informal History* (New York: Orbis Books, 1990).

78. Louis Cantor, *A Prologue to the Protest Movement*, 25.

79. Ibid., 25–26.

80. This does not mean that Union leaders were not honest in wanting to solve the immediate need of the rank and file. They undoubtedly were.

81. Statement of the STFU, Presented to the President's Special Committee on Farm Tenancy, Meeting at Dallas, Texas, January 4, 1937, *STFU* Reel four.

82. "Program of the Southern Tenant Farmers' Union of Oklahoma" March 1937, *STFU* Reel four.

83. Ibid., "Report on STFU convention," 1938, *STFU* Reel nine.

84. STFU in the News, January 7, 1967, *News* Reel c.

85. A New Policy and Program for the Southern Tenant Farmers' Union, 1941, *STFU* Reel seventeen.

EPILOGUE

1. Donald Grubbs, *Cry From The Cotton*, 192.

2. Woody Guthrie, "Dust Bowl Ballads," *Folkways Albums* No. FH5212, New York: Folkway Records, 1964.

BIBLIOGRAPHY

PRIMARY SOURCES

William Amberson Papers, Memphis University Special Collections

Arkansas Gazette

Caldwell, Erskine and Margaret Bourke-White. *You Have Seen Their Faces.* New York: Modern Age Books, Inc., 1937.

Daniels, Jonathan. *A Southerner Discovers the South.* New York: The Macmillan Company, 1938.

Theodore Draper Papers, Emory University

Clay East Papers, University of Arkansas

Kester, Howard A., *Howard A. Kester Papers 1923–1972.* Glen Rock, N. J.: Microfilming Corporation of America.

Marked Tree Tribune [Marked Tree, Arkansas]

Mitchell, H. L., *Green Rising: A Supplement to the* STFU *Papers, 1910–1977.* Glen Rock, N. J.: Microfilming Corporation of America, 1978.

Mitchell, H. L., *Official Papers of the Southern Tenant Farmers' Union.* Ann Arbor, Mich.: University Microfilms, 1973.

National Emergency Council. *Report on the Economic Conditions of the South.* Washington D.C.: Government Printing Office, 1938.

The Parkin Times [Parkin Arkansas]

Public Affairs Committee. *Farm Policies Under the New Deal.* New York: Public Affairs Committee, Inc., 1938

Southern Tenant Farmer's Union Scrapbook and Newspaper Clippings, 1934–1970. Chapel Hill: University of North Carolina Library, 1971–73.

Norman Thomas Papers, Cambridge: Chadwyck-Healey, 1985

United States Department of Agriculture. *Yearbook of Agriculture 1936.* 74th Congress, 2nd Session, House Document No. 338.

United States Department of Commerce. *Tenth Census of the United States: 1880*. Washington D. C.: Government Printing Office, 1882.

———. *Eleventh Census of the United States: 1890*. Washington D. C.: Government Printing Office, 1892.

———. *Twelfth Census of the United States: 1900*. Washington D. C.: Government Printing Office, 1902.

———. *Thirteenth Census of the United States: 1910*. Washington D. C.: Government Printing Office, 1912.

———. *Fourteenth Census of the United States: 1920*. Washington D. C.: Government Printing Office, 1922.

———. *Fifteenth Census of the United States: 1930*. Washington D. C.: Government Printing Office, 1932.

———. *Sixteenth Census of the United States: 1940*. Washington D. C.: Government Printing Office, 1942.

———. *Seventeenth Census of the United States: 1950*. Washington D. C.: Government Printing Office, 1952.

Henry A. Wallace Papers at the University of Iowa. Washington DC: National Historical Publications Commissions, 1974.

SECONDARY SOURCES

Agee, James and Walter Evans. *Let Us Now Praise Famous Men*. Boston: Houghton Mifflin Company, 1988.

Alexander, Donald Crichton. *The Arkansas Plantation*. New Haven: Yale University Press, 1943.

Altenbaugh, Richard J. *Education for Struggle: The American Labor Colleges of the 1920s and 1930s*. Philadelphia: Temple University Press, 1990.

Ameringer, Oscar. *If You Don't Weaken: The Autobiography of Oscar Ameringer*. Norman: The University of Oklahoma Press, 1983.

Arkansas Writers' Project. *Arkansas Times: A History of Arkansas*. Little Rock: Arkansas Writer's Project, Inc., 1994.

Ashmore, Harry S. *Arkansas: A History*. New York: W. W. Norton and Company, 1984.

Auerbach, Jerold S. "Southern Tenant Farmers: Socialist Critics of the New Deal." *Labor History* 7 (Winter, 1966).

Ayers, Edward L. *The Promise of the New South: Life After Reconstruction.* New York: Oxford University Press, 1992.

Baskett, Tom Jr., ed. *The Arkansas Delta: A Landscape of Change.* Helena, Ar.: Delta Cultural Center, 1990.

Berlin, Ira, et. al. *Slaves No More: Three Essays in Emancipation and the Civil War.* Cambridge: Cambridge University Press, 1990.

Bernstein, Irving. The Lean Years: *A History of the American Worker,* 1920–1933. New York: Da Capo Press, Inc., 1960.

Berry, Fred and John Novak, *The History of Arkansas.* Little Rock: Rose Publishing Company, 1987.

Biles, Rogers. *The South and the New Deal.* Lexington: The University Press of Kentucky, 1994.

———. *Memphis in the Great Depression.* Knoxville: The University of Tennessee Press, 1986.

Bode, Frederick A. and Donald E. Ginter. *Farm Tenancy and the Census in Antebellum Georgia.* Athens: The University of Georgia Press, 1986.

Boling, David. "Sharecroppers for Civil Liberties." *Southern Historian* 10 (1989).

Brinkley, Alan. *Voices of Protest: Huey Long, Father Coughlin, and the Great Depression.* New York: Vintage Books, 1983.

Buechner, Frederick, *The Alphabet of Grace.* San Francisco: Harper San Francisco, 1970.

Buhle, Mari Jo, Paul Buhle, and Dan Georgakas. *Encyclopedia of the American Left.* Urbana: University of Illinois Press, 1992.

Buhle, Mari Jo, Paul Buhle, and Harvey J. Kaye, ed. *The American Radical.* New York: Routledge, 1994.

Buhle, Paul, *Marxism in the United States: Remapping the History of the American Left,* London: Verso, 1991.

———. *A Dreamer's Paradise Lost: Louis C. Frania/Lewis Corey (1892–1953) and the Decline of Radicalism in the United States.* New Jersey: Humanities Press, 1995.

Cantor, Louis, *A Prologue to the Protest Movement.* Durham: Duke University Press, 1969.

Cantor, Milton. *The Divided Left: American Radicalism, 1900–1975.* New York: Hill and Wang, 1978.

Clark, Thomas D. *The Emerging South: A Study of the Social and Economic Revolution Which has Occurred in the South Since 1920*. New York: Oxford University Press, 1961.

Cobb, James C. and Michael V. Namorato, Eds. *The New Deal and the South*. Jackson: University Press of Mississippi, 1984.

Cohen, David. *The Life and Times of King Cotton*. New York: Oxford University Press, 1956.

Cohen, Robert, *When the Old Left Was Young*. New York: Oxford University Press, 1993.

Conkin, Paul K. *The New Deal*. New York: Thomas Y. Crowell Company, 1967.

Conrad, David Eugene, *The Forgotten Farmer: The Story of Sharecroppers in the New Deal*. Urbana: University of Illinois Press, 1965.

Cort, John C. *Christian Socialism: An Informal History*. New York: Orbis Books, 1990.

Craig, Robert H. *Religion and Radical Politics*. Philadelphia: Temple University Press, 1992.

Crews, Harry. A *Childhood: The Biography of a Place*. New York: Quill, 1983.

Daniel, Pete. *Breaking the Land:* The *Transformation of Cotton, Tobacco, and Rice Cultures Since 1880*. Urbana: University of Illinois Press, 1985.

——. *The Shadow of Slavery: Peonage in the South, 1901–1969*. Urbana: University of Illinois Press, 1985.

——. *Standing at the Crossroads: Southern Life in the Twentieth Century*. New York: Hill and Wang, 1986.

Davis, Ronald L. F. *Good and Faithful Labor: From Slavery to Sharecropping in the Natchez District, 1860–1890*. Westport: Greenwood Press, Inc., 1982.

Diggins, John Patrick. *The Rise and Fall of the American Left*. New York: W. W. Norton and Company, 1992.

Draper, Theodore. *American Communism and Soviet Russia*. New York: Vintage Books, 1960.

Dunbar, Anthony. *Against the Grain: Southern Radicals and Prophets, 1929–1959*. Charlottesville: University Press of Virginia, 1981.

Edegerton, John, *Speak Now Against the Day: The Generation Before the Civil Rights Movement in the South*. New York: Alfred A. Knopf, 1994.

Faulkner, William. *The Wild Palms*. New York: Vintage Books, 1966.

Fields, Barbara Jeanne. *Slavery and Freedom on the Middle Ground: Maryland During the Nineteenth Century*. New Haven: Yale University Press, 1985.

Fink, Gary M. and Merl E. Reed, Eds. *Race, Class, and Community in Southern Labor History*. Tuscaloosa: The University of Alabama Press, 1994.

Fink, Leon. *Workingmen's Democracy: The Knights of Labor and American Politics*. Urbana: University of Illinois Press, 1985.

Fite, Gilbert C. *Cotton Fields No More: Southern Agriculture, 1865–1980*. Lexington: University of Kentucky Press, 1984.

——. *George N. Peck and the Fight for Farm Parity*. Norman: The University of Oklahoma Press, 1954.

Flynt, Wayne. *Poor But Proud: Alabama's Poor Whites*. Tuscaloosa: The University of Alabama Press, 1989.

——. "One in Spirit, Many in Flesh: Southern Evangelicals," in David E. Harrell, Jr., ed., *Varieties of Southern Evangelicalism*. Macon: Mercer University Press, 1981

Foner, Eric. *Nothing but Freedom: Emancipation and Its Legacy*. Baton Rouge: Louisiana State University Press, 1983.

——. *Reconstruction: America's Unfinished Revolution, 1863–1877*. New York: Harper and Row, Pub., 1988.

Foner, Philip S. *The Workingmen's Party of the United States: A History of the First Marxist Party in the Americas*. Minneapolis: MEP Publications, 1984.

——. Proceedings of the Black National and State Conventions, 1865–1900. Philadelphia: Temple University Press, 1975.

——. The *Social Writings of Jack London*. Secaucus: Citadel Press, 1964 [1947].

——. *We The Other People: Alternative Declarations of Independence by Labor Groups, Farmers, Women's Rights Advocates, Socialists, and Blacks 1829–1975*. Urbana: University of Illinois Press, 1976.

Frey, Fred C. and T. Lynn Smith. "The Influence of the AAA Cotton Program Upon the Tenant, Cropper, and Laborer." *Rural Sociology* 1 (1936): 483–505.

Glymph, Thavolia, et. Al. *Essays in the Postbellum Southern Economy*. College Station: Texas A&M University Press, 1985.

Goodwyn, Lawrence. *Democratic Promise: The Populist Movement in America*. New York: Oxford University Press, 1976.

———. "The Cooperative Commonwealth and other Abstractions: In Search of a Democratic Promise." *Marxist Perspectives* 3 (2) (1980).

Graham, John, ed., *"Yours for the Revolution: The Appeal to Reason, 1895–1922.* Lincoln: University of Nebraska Press, 1990.

Green, James R. *Grass-Roots Socialism: Radical Movements in the Southwest, 1895–1943.* Baton Rouge: Louisiana State University Press, 1978.

Grubbs, Donald H. *Cry From the Cotton: The Southern Tenant Farmers' Union and the New Deal.* Chapel Hill: The University of North Carolina Press, 1971.

Guthrie, Woody. *Seeds of Man.* New York: E. P. Dutton and Co., Inc., 1976.

Gutman, Herbert G. and Donald H. Bell, ed., *The New England Working Class and the New Labor History.* Urbana: University of Illinois Press, 1987

Hahn, Steven. *The Roots of Southerner Populism: Yeoman Farmers and the Transformation of the Georgia Upcountry, 1850–1890.* New York: Oxford University Press, 1983.

Hall, Jacquelyn Dowd, et. al. *Like a Family: The Making of a Southern Cotton Mill World.* Chapel Hill: The University of North Carolina Press, 1987.

Hall, Robert L. and Carol B. Stack, ed. *Holding on to the Land and the Lord: Kinship, Ritual, Land, Tenure, and Social Policy in the Rural South.* Athens: The University of Georgia Press, 1982.

Hamilton, C. Horace. "The Social Effects of Recent Trends in the Mechanization of Agriculture." *Rural Sociology* 4 (1939).

Higgs, Robert. *Competition and Coercion: Blacks in the American Economy, 1865–1914.* Cambridge: Cambridge University Press, 1977.

Holly, Donald. *Uncle Sam's Farmers: The New Deal Communities in the Lower Mississippi Valley.* Urbana: University of Illinois Press, 1975.

Howe, Irving. *Socialism and America.* New York: Harcourt Brace Jovanovich, Publishers, 1985.

Howe, Irving and Lewis Coser. *The American Communist Party: A Critical History.* New York: Frederick A. Praeger, Pub., 1957.

Isserman, Maurice. *Which Side Were You On?: The American Communist Party During the Second World War.* Urbana: University of Illinois Press, 1993.

Kelly, Robin D. G. *Hammer and the Hoe: Alabama Communists During the Great Depression.* Chapel Hill: The University of North Carolina Press, 1990.

Kester, Howard. *Revolt Among The Sharecroppers.* New York: Arno press, 1969.

Kirby, Jack Temple. *Rural Worlds Lost: The American South, 1920–1960*. Baton Rouge: Louisiana State University Press, 1987.

Kiser, G. Gregory. "The Socialist Party in Arkansas, 1900–1912" Arkansas *Historical Quarterly* 40 (Summer 1981).

Klehr, Harvey. *The Heyday of American Communism: The Depression Decade*. New York: Basic Books, 1984.

Kruefer, Thomas A. *And Promises to Keep: The Southern Conference for Human Welfare, 1938–1948*. Nashville: Vanderbilt Press, 1967.

Laurie, Bruce. *Artisans Into Workers: Labor in Nineteenth Century America*. New York: The Noonday Press, 1989.

Lomax, Alan. *The Land Where the Blues Began*. New York: Bantam Doubleday Dell Publishing Group, Inc., 1993.

Maharidge, Dale and Michael Williamson. *And Their Children After Them*. New York: Random House, Inc. 1993.

Mandle, Jay R. *Not Slave, Not Free: The African American Economic Experience Since the Civil War*. Durham: Duke University Press, 1992.

Martin, Robert F. *Howard Kester and the Struggle for Social Justice in the South, 1904–77*. Charlottesville: University of Virginia Press, 1991.

McElvaine, Robert S., ed. *Down and Out in the Great Depression: Letters From the Forgotten Man*. Chapel Hill: The University of North Carolina Press, 1983.

Mertz, Paul E. *New Deal Policy and Southern Rural Poverty*. Baton Rouge: Louisiana State University Press, 1978.

Millcent, R. A *Touch of Newton County*. Los Angeles: Harbor House, Pub., 1963.

Miller, Marc S., ed. *Working Lives: The Southern Exposure History of Labor in the South*. New York: Pantheon Books, 1980.

Mitchell, H. L. *Mean Things Happening in this Land: The Life and Times of H. L. Mitchell Cofounder of the Southern Tenant Farmers' Union*. Montclair: Allanheld, Osmun, 1979.

Moneyhon, Carl H. *Arkansas and the New South, 1874–1929*. Fayetteville: The University of Arkansas Press, 1997.

Moore Jr., Winfreed and Joseph F. Tripp. *Looking South: Chapters in the Story of an American Region*. Westport: Greenwood Press, Inc., 1989.

Myrdal, Gunnar. *An American Dilemma: The Negro Problem and Modern Democracy*. New York: Harper and Row, Pub., 1962 [1944].

Naison, Mark D. "The Southern Tenant Farmers' Union and the CIO." *Radical America* 2 (1968): 36–56.

Nieman, Donald, ed. *From Slavery to Sharecropping: White Land and Black Labor in the Rural South, 1865–1900*. New York: Garland Press, 1994.

Ottanelli, Fraser M. *The Communist Party of the United States: From Depression to World War II*. New Brunswick: Rutgers University Press, 1991.

Randall, Willard Sterne. *Thomas Jefferson: A Life*. New York: Henry Holt and Company, 1993.

Ransom, Roger L. and Richard Sutch. *One Kind of Freedom: The Economic Consequences of Emancipation*. Cambridge University Press, 1977.

Raper, Arthur F. *Preface to Peasantry*. New York: Athenaeum, 1968.

Raper, Arthur F. and Ira DeA. Reid. *Sharecroppers All*. Chapel Hill: The University of North Carolina Press, 1941.

Rawick, George P. *The American Slave: A Composite Autobiography Series Two, Volume Seven*. Westport: Greenwood Press, Inc., 1972.

Reed, Roy. *Faubus: The Life and Times of an American Prodigal*. Fayetteville: The University of Arkansas Press, 1997.

Reidy, Joseph P. *From Slavery to Agrarian Capitalism in the Cotton Plantation South: Central Georgia, 1800–1880*. Chapel Hill: The University of North Carolina Press, 1992.

Richards, Henry I., *Cotton and the AAA*. Washington D. C.: The Brookings Institution, 1941.

Rochester, Anna. *Why Farmers Are Poor: The Agricultural Crisis in the United States*. New York: International Publishers, 1940.

Rosengarten, Theodore, *All God's Dangers: The Life of Nate Shaw*. New York: Vintage Books, 1974.

Rosenman, Samuel L. *The Public Papers and Addressees of Franklin D. Roosevelt*. 5 vols. New York: Random House, 1938.

Saloutos, Theodore. *Farmer Movements in the South, 1865–1933*. Lincoln: University of Nebraska Press, 1960.

——. *The American Farmer and the New Deal*. Ames: The Iowa University Press, 1982.

Salvatore, Nick. *Eugene V. Debs: Citizen and Socialist*. Urbana: University of Illinois Press, 1982.

Saville, Julie. *The Work of Reconstruction: From Slave to Wage Labor in South Carolina, 1860–1870*. New York: Cambridge University Press, 1994.

Schlesinger, Arthur M. Jr. *The Coming of the New Deal*. Boston: Houghton Mifflin Company, 1959.

Schulman, Bruce J. *From Cotton Belt to Sunbelt: Federal Policy, Economic Development, and the Transformation of the South, 1938–1980*. New York: Oxford University Press, 1991.

Shannon, David A. *The Socialist Party of America*. Chicago: Quadrangle Paperbacks, 1967.

Shannon, Fred A. *American Farmers' Movements*. Princeton, N. J.: D. Van Nostrand Company, Inc., 1957.

Shlomowitz, Ralph. "The Origins of Southern Sharecropping," *Agricultural History*, 53 (July 1979): 557–75.

Shore, Elliott. *Talkin' Socialism: J. A. Wayland and the Role of the Press in American Radicalism, 1890–1912*. Lawrence: University Press of Kansas, 1988

Stockley, Grif. *Blood In Their Eyes: The Elaine Race Massacres of 1919*. Fayetteville: The University of Arkansas Press, 2001.

Stokes, Melvyn and Rick Halpern, Eds. *Race and Class in the American South Since 1890*. Oxford: Berg, 1994.

Swanberg, W. A. *Norman Thomas: The Last Idealist*. New York: Charles Scribner's Sons, 1976.

Talbert, Roy Jr. *FDR's Utopian: Arthur Morgan of the TVA*. Jackson: University Press of Mississippi, 1987.

Thomas, Norman. *America's Way Out: A Program for Democracy*. New York: The Macmillan Company, 1931.

———. *As I See It*. New York: The Macmillan Company, 1932.

———. *The Choice Before Us*. New York: Arno Press, 1970.

———. *Human Exploitation*. New York: Frederick A. Stokes Co., 1934.

———. *A Socialists Faith*. New York: W.W. Norton & Co., 1951.

Thrasher, Sue and Leah Wise. *No More Moanin': Voices of the Southern Struggle*. Chapel Hill: The Institute for Southern Studies, 1974.

Tindall, George B. *The Emergence of The New South, 1913–1945*. Baton Rouge: Louisiana State University Press, 1967.

Venkataramani, M. S. "Norman Thomas, Arkansas Sharecroppers, and the Roosevelt Agricultural Policies, 1933–1937." *Mississippi Valley Historical Review* 47 (September 1960).

Weinstein, James. *The Decline of Socialism in America: 1912–1925*. New Jersey: Rutgers University Press, 1984 [1967].

Wharton, Vernon Lane. *The Negro in Mississippi, 1865–1890*. New York: Harper and Row, Publishers, 1947.

Whayne, Jeannie M., ed. *Shadows Over Sunnyside: An Arkansas Plantation in Transition, 1830–1945*. Fayetteville: The University of Arkansas Press, 1993.

Whayne, Jeannie M. and Willard B. Gatewood. *The Arkansas Delta: Land of Paradox*. Fayetteville: The University of Arkansas Press, 1993.

White, Graham and John Maze. *Wallace: Henry A. Wallace His Search for a New World Order*. Chapel Hill: University of North Carolina Press, 1995.

Wiener, Jonathan M. *Social Origins of the New South: Alabama, 1860–1885*. Baton Rouge: Louisiana State University Press, 1978.

Willens, Doris. *Lonesome Traveler: The Life of Lee Hays*. New York: W. W. Norton & Co., 1988.

Woodman, Harold D. New South, New Law: The *Legal Foundations of the Credit and Labor Relations I the Postbellum South*. Baton Rouge: Louisiana State University Press, 1995.

Woodward, C. Vann. *Origins of the New South, 1877–1913*. Baton Rouge: Louisiana State University Press, 1990.

Woofter, T. J. Jr., *Landlord and Tenant on the Cotton Plantation*. Washington DC: Works Project Administration, 1936.

Woofter T. J. Jr. and Ellen Winter. *Seven Lean Years*. New York: Da Capo Press, 1972 [1939].

Wright, Gavin. *Old South, New South: Revolutions in the Southern Economy Since the Civil War*. New York: Basic Books, 1986.

INDEX